Praise for
Kids Deali

T0063881

"If you are a preteen or teenager who is dealing with anxiety and how to follow Jesus at the same time, this devotional is for you. The text is easy-to-read and practical. Each devotional will help you go deep into the tough issues of life, if you allow the Scripture and Justine's words to settle into your soul. I have no doubt the Lord will meet you on every page."

—JUDY WEST, PASTOR/STAFF & LEADERSHIP
DEVELOPMENT AT THE CROSSING, ST. LOUIS, MO

"Justine Froelker is thoughtful, wise, and devoted to helping all of us live empowered lives. I felt so much peace reading each passage. The powerful devotions in Justine Froelker's devotional aimed at our youth are the words kids need to hear. She helps shepherd these young sheep as they learn to lean on God with all their emotions so they can love themselves and others well."

—SARAH PHILPOTT, AWARD-WINNING AUTHOR OF *LOVED BABY: 31 DEVOTIONS HELPING YOU GRIEVE, CHERISH YOUR CHILD AFTER PREGNANCY LOSS* AND *THE GROWING SEASON: A YEAR OF DOWN-ON-THE-FARM DEVOTIONS*

100 Devotions for Kids Dealing with Anxiety offers a composite of Scriptures, reflective thoughts, questions to consider, and journaling prompts about the struggle and reality of anxiety. As you walk through life with anxious moments or a cloud of anxiety, the daily reflections invite you to consider an optional way of looking at life. Justine Froelker gives readers a clearer understanding of the beauty that lies within their hearts as they sit with God's tender love.

—DIANNE MORRIS JONES, LPC, CDWF, AUTHOR OF *STOP BREATHE BELIEVE: MINDFUL LIVING ONE THOUGHT AT A TIME* AND *I'M FINE: A REAL FEELINGS JOURNAL*

"As a kid, I struggled with anxiety. I didn't have a name for those feelings, and I didn't have someone to help me process the big emotions. As an adult, while also parenting children who experience anxiety, I'm now learning to unravel all of this. *100 Devotions for Kids Dealing with Anxiety* allows us to have conversations organically while reading the devotions. Sometimes I don't have the right words to comfort them, but reading a devotional together and praying helps tremendously."

—KRISTEN HANFF, WRITER, ENTREPRENEUR, AND HOMESCHOOL MOM OF FOUR

"I just finished reading *100 Devotions for Kids Dealing with Anxiety*, and I am in awe. The book is incredible! Justine makes it so easy to break down Scripture and apply it to real-life while outlining action items to help our children work through their difficulties by making them identify and do the work."

—JENNIFER BARDOT, VP, SENIOR BUSINESS BANKER, ENTERPRISE BANK & TRUST

"Justine steps into vulnerability with authenticity. In this 100-day devotional, Justine discusses her journey with anxiety so she can build an authentic connection with the reader."

"This incredible devotional provides readers with a resource to create freeing practices and healthy behaviors to cope with anxiety. Justine teaches on the power of surrender and stillness, suggests practical ways you can learn to sit quietly and give yourself permission to feel. More importantly, Justine helps readers live with anxiety and acknowledge that these feelings are real, but the feelings don't define or control us. Anxious thoughts can crowd your mind and steal your joy. When we recognize this, we can use the practices Justine shares to "empty" our anxious mind and allow God's love to fill us. Even though this devotional is written for kids, there are so many helpful Scripture references and daily practices that anyone coping with anxiety will find beneficial."

"Justine's ability to bring Scripture into everyday life for kids is remarkable. Children of all ages will not only feel the loving arms of God around them while reading this devotional, but they will also come away with practical steps to use in their day-to-day lives to help with their anxiety. Justine does an amazing job of reminding the reader that God is right there with them, even if they don't always feel Him."

"Justine has provided families with a gift in this devotional—Scripture verses paired with practical steps of reflection and application. I cried the first time I read *100 Devotions for Kids Dealing with Anxiety*. While I try to speak words of life and encouragement over my children in the throes of anxious moments, their battle is not mine, and sometimes my words come up short. Justine's words have given us the language we need to better navigate this anxiety journey with Jesus at the center and understanding as our greatest tool. This book is a must-have resource for every parent of faith."

—REBECCA PIERCE, AUTHOR OF *DO TODAY WELL: GRACE-BASED STRATEGIES FOR PARENTING, MARRIAGE, FAITH & LIFE*

"I cannot wait to get this amazing devotional into the hands of children. At our counseling practice and grief center, we work with hundreds of children struggling with anxiety. Justine hears the hearts of struggling kids, provides practical tools through Scripture, and offers words of hope that things can be better."

—BEVERLY ROSS, MA, LPC-S, FOUNDER AND EXECUTIVE DIRECTOR OF WISE COUNTY CHRISTIAN COUNSELING & JENNY'S HOPE

"*100 Devotions for Kids Dealing with Anxiety* is a gift to children everywhere. As a mother to four sons, I find Justine's writing to be both comforting and practical. Justine offers a sense of belonging even in hard times and gives hope through practical steps our children can take to move through their anxious thoughts and feelings."

—MEG BROWN, VICE PRESIDENT OF HUMAN RESOURCES AT CAMBRIDGE AIR SOLUTIONS AND MOTHER OF FOUR SONS

"Justine gently leads her young readers to consider their feelings about the person of Jesus. Her thoughtful questions probe new ways to think about your life and offer simple actions you can take to feel better in a complicated and stressful world. Her journaling prompts offer a constructive way to process some of the struggles of growing up in today's world."

—FRAN CARADONNA, CHIEF EXECUTIVE OFFICER
AT SCHLAFLY BEER, SEEKER, AND MOM

"For someone who personally deals with anxiety and has an anxious five-year-old, *100 Devotions for Kids Dealing with Anxiety* has truly been a helpful everyday tool for us to use together. Working through the book with my daughter and reviewing each daily prompt has allowed us to think of ways to find meaning, purpose, and gratitude so we can better understand what she is experiencing and how we will show up in the world each day. This gentle and thoughtfully written devotional is a lovely reminder of how much we are loved. This book needs to be in every family's home."

—MARILYN GOMEZ, ENTREPRENEUR AND MILA'S MOM

"This devotional is filled with insights and reflections for all ages, especially tweens and teens. Justine has a beautiful and impactful way of imparting great wisdom in bite-sized chunks. Her reflection prompts are encouraging and support kids searching for their unique identity and purpose. *100 Devotions for Kids Dealing with Anxiety* is an incredible tool to connect with your child, grow in faith together, and support their identity development."

—KATE TURNER, THIRD PARTY AT RISK AT FIRST BANK AND MOTHER

"I wish I had this book when I was a child. Even as a grown-up, I find it quite beneficial. *100 Devotions for Kids Dealing with Anxiety* allows one to deepen their understanding of themselves and while doing so, deepen their connection to God and others. I highly recommend parents, relatives, and friends go through this book with their teens. The Bible verses are comforting, and the guided questions allow deeper reflection. Justine has written this in a way that will make everyone feel seen and understood."

—JANET PETRIE, PEOPLE AND CULTURE EXECUTIVE AND ENTHUSIAST

Justine created 100 bite-sized reminders of what's truly important for each of us, regardless of age or circumstance. She reminds us of our need for courage, vulnerability, and self-compassion. She reminds us to love and seek a higher purpose. *100 Devotions for Kids Dealing with Anxiety* challenges us to sit with our emotions by truly being present. I'm grateful for Justine's unique mixture of intellect, passion, and grace, as it's just what our messy, complicated world needs as we remember that we are enough. Whether you are young or old, struggle with anxiety, or are simply trying to get by in the complexity of our world at large, this book is the deep breath you need to find your way.

—BARRY ENGELHARDT, PROGRAM DIRECTOR, HEROIC
FORCES AT BOOTS TO BOOKS PROGRAM, AND HR
MANAGER AT STORE SUPPLY WAREHOUSE

I cannot wait to see the power and impact this 100-day devotional will have. So much of our world tells children they can't, they're not enough, or they need to do more. This devotional breaks down those lies while applying Scripture into practical and relatable nuggets of encouragement for real-life issues. *100 Devotions for Kids Dealing with Anxiety* is a powerful tool that will change the outlook for our children. I cannot wait to share this book with the tweens and teens in my life.

—JAYLENE KUNZE, CHIEF FINANCIAL OFFICER
AT UPLIGHT AND MOM OF TWO

100
devotions FOR kids
dealing with anxiety

100

devotions FOR kids

dealing with anxiety

JUSTINE FROELKER

ZONDERkidz™

ZONDERKIDZ

100 Devotions for Kids Dealing with Anxiety

Copyright © 2022 by Zondervan

Readers are urged to seek appropriate medical advice for anxiety and other serious health issues.

Requests for information should be addressed to:
Zonderkidz, *3900 Sparks Dr. SE, Grand Rapids, Michigan 49546*

ISBN 978-0-310-14064-1 (softcover)
ISBN 978-0-310-14065-8 (ebook)
ISBN 978-0-310-14077-1 (audio)

Content written and adapted by Justine Froelker.

Zonderkidz is a trademark of Zondervan.

Zondervan titles may be purchased in bulk for educational, business, fundraising, or sales promotional use. For information, please email SpecialMarkets@Zondervan.com.

Library of Congress Cataloging-in-Publication Data on File

Printed in the United States of America

22 23 24 25 26 LSC 6 5 4 3 2 1

Introduction

Dear friend,

I am honored to be writing this book for you, the teen I may never know in person—and yet I feel like I can guide and walk alongside you, with Jesus, to help you cope with anxiety.

It is my hope and prayer that over the next one hundred days, you will find the space to feel the calm and comfort of Jesus, identify the skills and resources to help you know that you are not your anxiety, and most of all feel God's love.

I'm here to help you—whether you need tools to help you fall asleep at night, strategies to calm the feeling when you can't catch your breath, or words to remind you that you are loved and that you matter. Throughout this book I will mostly write in the "we" perspective because we are in this together. Each day you will read a Scripture verse and a short devotional, followed by a journaling activity prompt, which is meant to help you move what you've read into your heart and practice. By being in community and connection with one another and with our Jesus, we heal. The world is hard and can be scary. When we have Jesus as our example, friend, and Savior through it, we know we are never alone.

Justine
Froelker

Day 1

Jesus often withdrew to lonely places and prayed.

LUKE 5:16

Some people like being alone more than others. Some of us love being around lots of people. And some of us are a little bit of both. Do you feel energized after spending time alone or after spending time around people? Sometimes it can feel like we are super connected, especially with the internet, FaceTime, and social media. However, there can be limitations to online connections because it means we are often missing the true presence of other people.

You know that presence where you can read someone's body language, see their facial expressions, look into their eyes, and even kind of feel their emotions and respond in real time? Although these things may be missing in online interactions, I have no doubt that true connection is still possible—if we are being our true, authentic selves. Either way, learning to sit with ourselves is a skill we must learn and one that Jesus demonstrated in Scripture. Like we see in today's verse, Jesus often sat by Himself, away from others, and turned to His Father. Sometimes it feels scary to sit with ourselves and be alone. Remember that alone doesn't necessarily mean lonely, especially because God is always with us whether we ask Him to be or not—although I think He likes it when we invite Him to be with us.

When you are alone, do you feel lonely? Does this bring up more anxiety for you? How can you turn to God with that anxious, lonely feeling?

_____

_____

_____

_____

_____

_____

_____

_____

_____

Day 2

Whether you turn to the right or to the left, your ears will hear a voice behind you, saying, "This is the way; walk in it."

ISAIAH 30:21

You know that voice inside of you, the one that always seems to be there, whether or not you want to listen to it? The voice may barely be a whisper some days. Other days, it is a booming voice that you simply cannot ignore. Some people refer to the voice as intuition or a gut instinct. For those of us who know who God is, we often call it Holy Spirit.

Maybe it is all of the above. Regardless, life will pull you in many directions. Maybe it is toward an opinion of someone you respect or an authority figure who has an opposing opinion. Perhaps your friends have changed interests and the things they like don't align with your interests or outlook anymore.

Somewhere inside, somewhere you can't quite name, you hear that voice, a whisper or a shout, that says, "This is the way; walk in it." The Hebrew word for *way* in this verse means road, much like the Greek word used in

John 14:6. Jesus said He is the way, the truth, and the life. The road in front of you has a guide that will walk alongside you and show you the way. You have to listen carefully so you can hear Him.

Is there something going on right now that is bringing you anxiety? What can you do today to get quiet enough to increase Holy Spirit's whisper to a shout?

_____

_____

_____

_____

_____

_____

_____

_____

_____

Day 3

Be still before the Lᴏʀᴅ and wait patiently for him.

PSALM 37:7

Between schoolwork, activities, clubs, and whatever else is on your plate you probably feel like there is never time for rest. You might even believe that rest is not productive or that doing nothing is bad. It is easy to look around and believe the only way to get something done or to feel better is to do it on your own.

What if the thing we need to do is simply to be still and wait, like in today's verse? More than that, what if we can learn to wait even if we aren't the most patient person? I know that our schedules and the world can make it seem like we aren't doing enough. However, many times Scripture says we need to be still and wait on God. Be still before the Lord. Maybe this means that in our stillness we'll find help. That in doing nothing we are actually being productive. Turn to God in the stillness. Maybe even ask Him to help you wait and provide the patience to be still.

When was the last time you were still and did nothing? Today set a timer for five minutes and ask God to join your stillness and strengthen your patience. During those five minutes focus on your breath, count the shades of green where you are, or read today's verse over and over. Did it get easier as you sat there in stillness?

_____

_____

_____

_____

_____

_____

_____

_____

_____

_____

_____

_____

Day 4

I have seen everything that is done under the sun, and
behold, all is vanity and a striving after wind.

ECCLESIASTES 1:14 ESV

Trophies, titles, teams, and your class schedule are all
very important things. But as today's verse says, could
they also be ways that we strive after the wind? What
does that even mean?

I know it can be hard to believe, and I need you to
know this: You are more than the trophies you've won,
the titles you have earned, the classes you take, the grades
you achieve, and whatever else you may be told make you
who you are. So much of life is striving to earn, please,
and be perfect in order to feel like we are okay, like we
matter, like we are enough. Except you do not have to
strive for enoughness. You are a child of God. You were
created in His image. You are enough.

The things you do and the things you work hard for
may be things that you enjoy, that you are good at, or that
you aren't very good at (and yet still enjoy). They aren't
who you are. These things help you show up in the world

as yourself, they help you connect with others, and they shape your interests. They don't make you enough. You already are.

Do you ever feel like the things that define you make you feel more anxious? Like they are no longer who you are or who you want to be? Today, pray for God to help you see and feel your enoughness outside of your activities.

_____

_____

_____

_____

_____

_____

_____

_____

_____

_____

Day 5

A generous person will prosper; whoever
refreshes others will be refreshed.

PROVERBS 11:25

Kindness is all the rage and yet sometimes it feels like
this world is anything but kind. It is true that our
words and actions have ripple effects beyond what we
can see. Just like when we throw a rock into a lake, the
ripples reach farther than we think possible. When we
give in a generous, kind, and altruistic way we know that
God will use that well beyond our imaginations. We can
also trust that somehow we will be refreshed ourselves.
Giving back is one of the best ways to navigate through
anxiety and depression.

Serving others helps us get out of our own feelings,
which can easily feel like too much some days. Anxiety
can quickly make things all about us. Our thoughts and
feelings can circle around and around and feel overwhelming. To show up in kindness for someone else can
break that cycle of anxiety. And like today's verse says, it
will fill us up too. Love, grace, and kindness are infinite

and only create more love, grace, and kindness. When you give, you're keeping your heart and eyes open enough to also receive all God has for you.

When was the last time you served someone else without expecting anything in return? What did that feel like? What small act of kindness can you do today?

_____

_____

_____

_____

_____

_____

_____

_____

_____

_____

_____

Day 6

The LORD make his face shine on you and be gracious to you;
the LORD turn his face toward you and give you peace.

NUMBERS 6:25–26

Sometimes God can be intimidating. Sometimes we may even feel a little scared of Him. He is the Creator of all things. There are some of those tougher stories we read, especially in the Old Testament, where His wrath is kind of frightening. Don't be fooled—even in those tougher stories, God's love, faithfulness, and grace are present.

Some of the greatest lies that anxiety tells us are that we aren't enough, that no one cares, that no one can help us, and that we are alone. None of this is true. You have a God who loves you. You have people who love you, who can and will help you. God's face shines on you with a grace that meets you where you are and lets you know that He is with you. Even on those tough days when you aren't turning toward Him, He will turn toward you. And not only will He turn toward you, meet you, and sit beside you with so much love, He will also give you peace. He gives you peace because He is peace. Even when you don't have peace because anxiety feels like it has stolen it, Jesus can and will be that peace.

If it is a sunny day and you can go outside, go ahead and do this exercise there. Allow your face to feel the warmth of the sun and take a deep breath. Otherwise, imagine that it is a beautiful, sunny day and you are sitting in its warmth.

Write down something you're struggling to find peace with. How will peace ease your anxiety? Now close your eyes and take a deep breath. Ask Jesus if today, even if only for this moment, He will be your peace and help you feel peace.

_____

_____

_____

_____

_____

_____

_____

_____

_____

Day 7

A heart at peace gives life to the body.

PROVERBS 14:30

The heart is our life source. Its job is to pump blood throughout the circulatory system. Blood carries oxygen and nutrients that all our organs need to stay healthy. Without the heart, there is no life. And then there's the not-so-sciencey stuff about the heart's connection to our mind, soul, emotions, and the essence of who we are. With everything going on in the world, it is difficult to keep our hearts at peace, especially when anxiety is high.

When this happens, it can sometimes feel as though our hearts care too much. There is so much to worry about, plan for, or fix. And nothing feels like peace. When you are in that place, and your heart feels anxious, your emotions can trigger intense reactions. You might find yourself yelling at people you love, struggling with schoolwork, or creating drama with your friends. We aren't supposed to worry about it all. We definitely don't have as much control as anxiety falsely leads us to believe. If we want our bodies to have life, our hearts must fight for, create, and receive peace.

Sometimes, a brain dump can really help your anxious heart and mind. Write down everything that you are worried about right now. This is not a permanent list. It is simply an exercise to get it out of your head and make these things a little less powerful. Once your list is complete, turn to God and ask Him if there is something on the list you need to tackle right now. If so, do it and set the rest of the list aside for now. When you feel anxious again, revisit your list and repeat this exercise.

_____

_____

_____

_____

_____

_____

_____

_____

_____

_____

Day 8

Do not worry about tomorrow.

MATTHEW 6:34

Anxiety often tricks us into believing that our worries about tomorrow will actually change tomorrow. In reality, all that anxiety and worry only steals our today.

Maybe you're dreading a test you have tomorrow and anxiety is tricking you into believing that worrying will help you do better. Rather, studying is the actual thing that will improve your grade. Worrying about tomorrow can feel like it is productive because it keeps our brains busy. But it doesn't really help us with tomorrow.

This is going to sound weird. One way to help your worries is to thank them. Give it a try. "Thank you worry. I know you are trying to help me through this anxiety. I've got this and God will help me. So I don't need you today." Another way to challenge the worries for tomorrow is to remind ourselves that today is a day that we have never lived. We will never get to live this day again. Be present now. Be here with Jesus. Take a breath and be.

What is something that is happening for you today that could be compromised by worrying about tomorrow?

_____

_____

_____

_____

_____

_____

_____

_____

_____

_____

_____

_____

_____

Day 9

In repentance and rest is your salvation, in
quietness and trust is your strength.

ISAIAH 30:15

It can often feel easier to retreat, suffer by ourselves, and
allow anxiety to tell us that we are alone. Sometimes anxiety
can stop us from turning to God. When we turn to God with
all of it—the good, the bad, the ugly, the anxious, and the
arrogant—we will find rest by sharing our burdens with Him.

It is in this connection with Him that we will find rest
and true meaning. When we live life through and because
of Jesus, it is easier to trust the victory He promises—the
victory we stand in because of the strength we find in our
faith and in who God is to us and who He tells us we are.
This trust we have in Him is our strength.

Being strong doesn't mean that we won't struggle, that
we'll do it all perfectly, or that life is easy and completely
anxiety-free. Through it all, God is our strength when we
believe what we read in Scripture. Rest, prayer, self-care,
and self-compassion are the skills that help us walk in that
strength daily.

What does salvation mean to you? You may not associate the words
quietness and trust with strength, even though you read them in
today's verse. How do you find strength in quietness and trust,
especially in your relationship with God? What are some ways you can
quietly trust God today and every day?

_____

_____

_____

_____

_____

_____

_____

_____

_____

_____

_____

Day 10

Do not worry about your life, what you will eat; or
about your body, what you will wear. For life is more
than food, and the body more than clothes.

LUKE 12:22–23

Some people may find today's verse easier to accept than others. For some it feels almost impossible not to worry about food or clothes because they don't know where their next meal is coming from or if they'll have clean clothes for school. For others it feels foreign because their fridges are full of food and their closet contains all their favorite clothes.

When Jesus told His disciples not to worry about their lives, He was referring to the greed and material possessions we all think about. Oftentimes, this material envy will lead us to a worrisome obsession over physical things, causing our identities to become wrapped up in those things.

You are more than the labels associated with having too much or not enough. Life is far more than the stuff we possess. I believe that because Jesus said so, and I believe

Him. Even though it may seem impossible, somehow God will always provide just enough. This is why Jesus said not to worry.

Sometimes it can be hard not to allow the material things to define us. If you're struggling with this, consider the following questions: Who are you outside of these things? What makes you who you are? Who were you created to be? If you need a little help, start with these things: loved, chosen, redeemed.

_____

_____

_____

_____

_____

_____

_____

_____

_____

Day 11

Such knowledge is too wonderful for me,
too great for me to understand!

PSALM 139:6 NLT

We just want to figure it out. We want life to be predictable. Just tell us what is going to happen and we will be able to figure out how to be, what to do, and how to feel. These are the lies of anxiety and society. Anxiety often makes us believe the story that we must try to figure out everything ourselves. An anxious mind often creates so many questions. *What is wrong with me? Why can't I just relax? Stop caring? What can I try next to fix me? Go to sleep already! Don't freak out! Why can't I _____?*

Part of the work of coping with our anxiety and doing it by faith means that we surrender having to know it all. We don't have to figure ourselves out. We don't need to be fixed! God loves everyone the same. He knitted us together and knew us before He gave us our first breaths. It is all far too wonderful and great for us to fully understand. Please know that you don't need to be fixed because you aren't actually broken. You simply need to feel loved. I know that some days it may be difficult to understand. I promise though, God loves you as you are right now. He's loved you all along, anxiety or no anxiety.

What does it feel like to know that you have a God who understands it all, beyond what you ever will? Write down some of the things you need to stop trying to figure out.

_____

_____

_____

_____

_____

_____

_____

_____

_____

_____

Day 12

Godliness with contentment is great gain.

1 TIMOTHY 6:6

Sometimes contentment can feel like a loaded word. Anxiety and the hustle ingrained in society can make us believe that contentment somehow means that we will become lazy or stop working hard to achieve things when we are satisfied with where we are.

What if contentment means that we can pause to enjoy where we are right now? During that pause, we can reflect and practice gratitude because we have everything we need in the moment. When we rely on God, we can trust that we have enough—and more than that, we are enough. To be surrendered in awe with trust and peace, especially when anxiety is trying to make us believe that it can be stolen, allows us to stand in the abundance and freedom that Jesus promised. Give yourself permission to feel content. If anxiety comes up and tells you *it is never enough, you have to do more*, stand tall and say, "My God is my peace. Anxiety, you aren't welcome here."

When was the last time you felt content? What are some ways you can relish in contentment? If you've never felt content, what do you think you need to feel it? Remember, you can ask God to help you feel and see contentment today. He will show up!

_____

_____

_____

_____

_____

_____

_____

_____

_____

_____

_____

_____

_____

Day 13

I have told you these things, so that in me you may
have peace. In this world you will have trouble.
But take heart! I have overcome the world.

JOHN 16:33

This is a verse full of promises—except one doesn't feel so
awesome. Jesus promised us that we will have trouble
in this life and world. Things will be tough sometimes.
Life won't seem fair. Anxiety will feel like it is taking over
your whole body. When you're feeling overwhelmed with
anxiety, remember Jesus' second promise. He told us that
He has overcome the world. We know He has won.

It might not feel like it, but somehow and someday
things will be okay. Even more than that, things will be
for our good and His glory.

Don't miss that sentence between the two promises
though. It doesn't say not to struggle since you know it
will be okay. Jesus said to take heart; in other translations
it says "be courageous." Choose courage.

Courage means more than bravery or heroics. According
to Dr. Brené Brown, courage means to tell the story of

who you are with your whole heart. I want you to tell your whole story—the troubles that Jesus promised us and the knowledge He put inside of you that victory is ours because of Him.

What are some of the troubles you are facing right now? Can you find evidence that helps you feel and see God's faithfulness and presence? Will you choose courage and feel both the trouble and the triumph? What does courage look like for you?

_____

_____

_____

_____

_____

_____

_____

_____

Day 14

The LORD does not look at the things people look at. People look at the outward appearance, but the LORD looks at the heart.

1 SAMUEL 16:7

It is so easy to get tripped up on how you look. Even though I believe technology and social media have negatively affected the way we view our appearances, I think they have provided freedom to express and explore how we want to look. People will almost always judge based on what they see. They will make up stories about who others are based on what they look like and what they wear. We must not hold those criticisms close to our hearts or conform to those judgments.

It is what is inside that matters most, especially to God. What if your appearance wasn't based on protecting yourself from judgment but rather displayed to the world who you are? To show the world the heart that God sees. Under it all, He knows you, He sees you, and He loves you. The hairs on your head, your thoughts—even the anxious thoughts—He sees, He knows, and He loves. You can't cover yourself up from your loving Father.

Knowing that God looks at and knows your heart, what does He see?
How could you show this to the world today?

_____

_____

_____

_____

_____

_____

_____

_____

_____

_____

_____

_____

Day 15

When anxiety was great within me,
your consolation brought me joy.

PSALM 94:19

Life can feel like a lot. So much to think about, to do, to figure out—and that's even without the times that we struggle with anxious thoughts and feelings. The racing thoughts, no thoughts, or the ruminating repetitive thoughts. There are so many ways our bodies may respond: a racing heart, a pounding heart, or the feeling of a weight on our chest. Many times, our stomachs churn or make weird noises or it feels like a brick is sitting inside. And then there's the breathing or lack thereof—like we can't catch a breath or take a deep breath. Our thoughts catastrophize and go through every worst-case scenario. There is worrying, overplanning, and excessive to-do lists. There are thoughts of perfection even though we know it isn't possible.

Anxiety in the really tough days feels massive. Like it consumes us. Like it is everything.

We have Psalm 94:19, which tells us that it is in these

very times that God's comfort and compassion can and will bring us joy. When life feels dark and full of anxiety, it is there in the shadow that God is closest to us. Which means we have His comfort and compassion. I wonder, if we allowed that to be enough, could we feel the joy that is promised in today's verse?

Think about one of the last times your anxiety felt overwhelming. Knowing what you know now, how would you have comforted yourself? When you think of God's comfort and compassion, what do you picture? Take some deep breaths and use this picture as a visualization the next time your anxiety ramps up.

_____

_____

_____

_____

_____

_____

_____

Day 16

The LORD is close to the brokenhearted
and saves those who are crushed in spirit.

PSALM 34:18

It is easy to allow anxiety to make us think that God doesn't care about our struggles and our heartbreaks. Sometimes it is even easy to believe that God caused our struggles and heartbreaks. One of the best things I learned that helped me with my own anxiety was to know and remember who God really is. To believe the character He shows us in Jesus. To believe His promises.

When I read Psalm 34:18 I find comfort knowing that God is close when we are struggling. I also know He knows the feeling of being brokenhearted because He lived as Jesus. Jesus felt grief. Jesus wept. Jesus felt the struggle of life in this world. He was man and God all at the same time, which is confusing and amazing and means that He is always close in our brokenheartedness. Knowing all that He would have to go through, He chose us. He knew and felt the crushing and He endured it to rescue us. That is how much He loves us. Don't let anxiety tell you that your God doesn't get it. He gets it. He gets you. He is close and He is always rescuing.

Have you ever thought about Jesus as the example of how we can endure struggle and heartbreak? What other characteristics of Jesus can you emulate in this life?

_____

_____

_____

_____

_____

_____

_____

_____

_____

_____

Day 17

Teach me knowledge and good judgment,
for I trust your commands.

PSALM 119:66

If we looked to Jesus as an example for how to live, I think many of our anxieties could be calmed. Jesus modeled how to love one another, how to set boundaries, how to take breaks and rest, and how to fight for and help those who are struggling. When we look to Jesus, we will find the knowledge and good judgment we need to live a life full of grace and love. Anxiety fools us into believing that life is all about the rules, the strivings, and earning God's love. This isn't the good life we read about in Scripture.

We must remember what Jesus said were His greatest commandments. Love God with all your heart and love His people. When we love God with all our hearts we will see reflected back to us, especially through the life of Jesus, that loving others is the good life. And you know what? I think that also means loving ourselves well. We cannot give what we don't have. To meet ourselves with the grace and love that Jesus loves us with is how we can live out His commandments and receive His good knowledge. It is love. It always comes back to love.

Anxiety will often tell you that love isn't enough. When anxiety creeps in, remember how much God loves you, how Jesus showed that love to people in Scripture, and then I want you to do something to show that love to yourself. Maybe it's watching a funny show, talking with your best friend, eating your favorite food, taking a walk, listening to music, or creating something amazing. Make a list of ways you can show love to yourself. Next time anxiety tries to steal your self-love, refer to this list and do something for yourself.

_____

_____

_____

_____

_____

_____

_____

Day 18

For from his fullness we have all received, grace upon grace.

JOHN 1:16 ESV

Grace can feel like such a big, tricky thing. The world tells us that we don't deserve it. If we know who Jesus is and believe that He suffered and died for us, then grace takes on an entirely different meaning. One of the best things I've ever read and learned is that Jesus looked at the cross and then back at us and still chose the cross. It is in His sacrifice that we received grace upon grace. The generosity of love. The benefit of the doubt. The gift that we are worth everything to our Creator. Everything.

I know it is hard to wrap our heads around being loved this much. I know that when our heads are spinning with worry and anxiety, it feels like it maybe isn't enough. What if you took some of that abundant grace—the grace upon grace—that you have because of Jesus and met yourself with it today?

What would it look like today if you met yourself with a little grace, especially knowing that you have grace upon grace through Jesus already? What could you do? How would that grace make a difference in your life? How could that grace make a difference in the lives of others?

_____

_____

_____

_____

_____

_____

_____

_____

_____

_____

_____

_____

Day 19

I pray that from his glorious, unlimited resources he will empower you with inner strength through his Spirit.

EPHESIANS 3:16 NLT

You know those days when you feel like you have nothing left to give? When it feels easier to not try, to not fight it, to just crawl under the covers and forget the worries, the assignments, the games, and everything else that the world needs from you? I know it seems unreal and not even possible to move forward. But what if that is anxiety making you feel that way?

After Jesus died on the cross for us, He came back and gifted us with Holy Spirit. Jesus told the disciples they would do far greater things than Him. He didn't just die to get us to heaven; He died to put heaven, Him, in us. Through Him we have strength. In Him we have His resources. Those unlimited resources do not have an expiration date and are limitless.

What are some of the glorious and unlimited resources you know come from God? That you've learned about Jesus? Make a list. What characteristics of His do you see and feel in you through Him?

_____

_____

_____

_____

_____

_____

_____

_____

_____

_____

_____

_____

_____

_____

Day 20

I come to you for shelter.
Protect me, keep me safe, and don't disappoint me.

PSALM 25:20 CEV

Picture this. The wind is howling, the sky is dark except for the flashes of lightning, which are preceded by roars of thunder. You know that you aren't going to make it to the overhang before the sky opens up with massive raindrops. Sometimes anxiety can feel like getting caught in a storm. So much is out of our control. We don't know how the wind will blow, and the crash of thunder makes us jump. The lightning is scary and we know the rain will be cold. What do we do?

We run for shelter. We don't walk, we don't stop along the way to take in the lightning—we run. We run because the shelter will provide protection and safety. Anxiety can make us believe that we can't run to God for shelter. Maybe our anxiety lies to us and tells us that God will be disappointed in us because anxiety has creeped in again. I want you to know that you can run to your shelter in God. He is a refuge; we can turn to Him with all the hard things and we will be protected. Run to Him!

What would it look like, in thoughts and behaviors, if you ran to God for shelter the next time your anxiety creeped in? Maybe prayer, dancing to music, singing really loud, or asking someone you trust for help. Write down what it would look like for you. How would running to God change the way you handle anxiety?

_____

_____

_____

_____

_____

_____

_____

_____

_____

_____

_____

_____

Day 21

I can do all things through him who strengthens me.

PHILIPPIANS 4:13 ESV

*Y*ou're so strong! You can do this! When people say those positive things to you, they are expressing support and maybe even admiration. Except, too often, it can feel like those sayings minimize how hard things actually are. Or even that someone isn't willing to sit beside you and imagine just how awful things are. You'll find oftentimes people don't understand anxiety—they won't try to—and instead they will attempt to cheer you through to the other side by telling you how strong you are. Plus, in our culture, strong often means not feeling the tougher emotions. Society sometimes implies that if you stop to feel how hard life is, especially with anxiety, then you are weak.

I'm going to be real with you. I don't want to be strong, and I am not going to cheerlead and call you strong either.

Resilient? Yes.

We are resilient when we choose to do the work to cope with our struggles and anxiety in a healthy way. We are resilient when we choose to do the things that help us sit with our anxiety. We are resilient when we remember that Christ is in us and that with Him we can do all things with His strength—not our own.

Sometimes I just wish we didn't have to be so darn resilient.

Looking back at some of the toughest seasons of your life, what were some of the things that helped you be resilient? How did relying on Jesus help you choose those things?

_____

_____

_____

_____

_____

_____

_____

_____

_____

Day 22

Cast all your anxiety on him because he cares for you.

1 PETER 5:7

Anxiety can be such a funny and annoying thing. It can come out of nowhere and for what seems like no reason. It can attach to the weirdest things. Maybe anxiety tells you that you have to do ten different things to be able to fall asleep. Maybe your anxiety is about something on the school bus. Or something you don't want to eat. Or maybe it's weird thoughts that are always there about your future.

I wonder, despite the silliness and odd attachment issues, if we can, like today's verse says, hand it over to Jesus. Even if only for a short time today. Name the anxiety. Consider writing it down. Not to make it a permanent record, just to get it out of your head and make it less powerful. Then hand it over to Him.

Ask Jesus to take it. *Lord, will You take it, even if just for a bit today?* Trust Him with it, so you can receive some peace and quiet. He cares. He can handle it and He can leave you with peace. He can even be your peace for a little while.

Write down some of your anxieties about today. Then close this book. Ask Jesus to take it for today. You aren't denying that it exists; you aren't pushing it away and pretending it is not there. You are simply asking Jesus to take it for a bit. It will be there tonight, if you really need to see the list again.

_____

_____

_____

_____

_____

_____

_____

_____

_____

_____

_____

Day 23

Cast your cares on the LORD and he will sustain you;
he will never let the righteous be shaken.

PSALM 55:22

H ere is that word again: "cast." In yesterday's verse, the
Greek word for *cast* means to throw upon. In today's
verse the Hebrew word for *cast* means "to throw out,
down, away." I've had days when I wanted to chuck my
anxiety to someone, something, anything! Here, in both
of these verses, we are told we can do just that, and onto
God nonetheless.

Imagine for a second our God, all powerful and all
loving, telling us, "Hey everyone, I am serious, throw it
to Me. Don't hold back. I know this is hard. I know this
sucks, and I can totally take it. Let Me have it."

In the verses we read, "cast" is followed by a promise.
He cares; He will sustain us and never let us be shaken.
Never. My anxiety easily forces me to not believe that
because sometimes anxiety literally makes me shake! And
still, somehow, we can rely on these Scriptures and promises. What would it be like to live these as fact? That we

can choose to surrender it, hand it over, and chuck it to God. Because then, maybe, just maybe, our hands are free enough to receive that care and sustenance that He promises.

What anxiety are you experiencing that feels too big for you? What would it feel like to chuck it to God, to let Him have it?

_____

_____

_____

_____

_____

_____

_____

_____

_____

_____

_____

Day 24

Do not be anxious about anything, but in every situation, by prayer and petition, with thanksgiving, present your requests to God.

PHILIPPIANS 4:6

Sometimes I feel like the Bible downright contradicts itself. I mean, earlier we talked about how Jesus promised us we would have trouble and then here we read to not be anxious about anything. I will admit, even as an adult, I want to be like, "Seriously, Dude! How can it be both?" (Yes, even when I call God Dude, I capitalize.) Then I remember, our brains are wired for story. Our brains make stuff up. When anxiety is sitting high, the stuff that our brains make up is usually pretty dramatic and inaccurate. And when we have anxiety sometimes, we catastrophize and dress-rehearse the worst-case scenario. We think it preps us for when the worst-case scenario happens. Except, it doesn't. All that worrying only steals our present moment. A moment that we have never lived before and will never live again.

When Paul wrote to the Philippians—and to us—to be anxious about nothing, he was reminding us that we have a tool to use. We have prayer with thanksgiving, basically gratitude. When we choose to find something to be grateful for it is not denying that things are hard or that we don't have a ton to worry about. It is simply reminding our brains that here in this present moment, we have something to be grateful for, and we have a God who will help us through it.

Today, a few times, maybe in the morning and then again before bed, make a gratitude list. What are you grateful for today? What are you grateful for about yourself? About school? About friends? Family? And of course, what are you grateful to God for?

_____

_____

_____

_____

_____

_____

_____

_____

Day 25

I praise you because I am fearfully and wonderfully made;
your works are wonderful, I know that full well.

PSALM 139:14

I find it helpful to remember the different meanings of *fearfully* in the Bible because the word shows up a lot and refers to different things. Honestly, being afraid of God doesn't help me feel like I can turn to Him with all my stuff, especially the hard stuff like anxiety. In this verse, the Hebrew meaning of fearfully is "to revere," which means a deep respect or even to be in awe of. When I remember that I was made to be in awe of who God is and how much He loves me, it helps me remember that He knows me, loves me, and that I can turn to Him with all of my life, most especially the really tough parts, like anxiety.

Each of us was made in awe and to awe. We are each known and made to be distinct and wonderful because we are one of God's great works. Can you imagine how anxiety would shrink if we remembered this more often? If we lived from this place—that there has never been another person on earth like you and there never will be again. So the next time anxiety tries to tell you that you aren't special, that you are nothing wonderful, you remember today's verse.

Try a prayer with this Scripture. Read this Scripture out loud several times. Each time you read it out loud, emphasize one word at a time, until you've read through it emphasizing each word. Sometimes I find this exercise helpful when I'm trying to get Scripture into my head, heart, and even bones. Repeating the verse helps me to hear the verse in different ways. After you're done, write down any thoughts you have.

_____

_____

_____

_____

_____

_____

_____

_____

Day 26

But even if you suffer for doing what is right, God will reward you for it. So don't worry or be afraid of their threats.

1 PETER 3:14 NLT

Anxiety often tells us to suffer alone, that no one will understand what we are going through, and that we can't reach out, ask for help, or tell someone what our anxious thinking is because they will think we are messed up or crazy. Which means our anxiety just spins on itself and grows. What we don't speak will fester. The unspoken is never benign.

I know anxiety tells you that it is wrong to speak, to reach out, and to tell someone what goes through your mind. You need to know that when you speak your truth, the dark gets less dark, and the light feels closer and warmer. According to today's verse, God will reward this. I love looking up the Greek and Hebrew meanings of the words in our daily verses, and of course, I needed to know what *reward* means. Because on the days where anxiety tells us to keep quiet and to suffer on our own, I think we need to be reminded that there is a reward in speaking up.

And wouldn't you know it, the Greek word for *reward* here means happy, blessed, and even supremely blessed. Wow, just wow! Today hold on to that. The suffering, especially when you speak it, can lead you to be happy and supremely blessed.

Today, can you reach out to someone you trust and tell them how you are doing? I mean, really tell them how you are, none of the fronting for an image, faking happy, or responding how you think you "should." Show up, all of you, and let that person love you. Write down who you talked to and how it felt to be honest with that person.

_____

_____

_____

_____

_____

_____

_____

_____

Day 27

Say to those who have an anxious heart, "Be strong; fear not!"

ISAIAH 35:4 ESV

When you first read today's verse, you may actually feel not so great. When someone tells us to just be strong, or not be fearful, it can feel like they are denying how hard things are. And I promise you, denying or plowing through anxiety is not helpful. In fact the more we deny it, push it down, and pretend it isn't there, the more it will fester, and eventually it will consume our identity.

We are not our anxiety. God did not give us an anxious heart. God is not the God of anxiety. What if the lesson of today's verse is to separate out our anxiety from our hearts? So, when you feel your anxiety, you can know that you have strength through Jesus and this is how you can be strong and not fear.

We are not our feelings. Lots of people choose to be their feelings. Lots of people choose to not cope with their emotions in a healthy way, which means their feelings own their voice. When we cope in a healthy way and know who we are in Christ, our feelings are not our identity. We can speak our feelings, cope with our feelings, and allow our feelings to move through. It is in this resilience practice that the words *"be strong"* and *"fear not"* stop feeling like a denial of our experience. God does not deny our feelings, our struggles, or our experience. He sees us, He is with us, and most of all He asks that we turn to Him through it all.

Today, take some time to write out "feeling" and "I am" statements. For example: I feel anxiety. I feel my heart racing. I feel my worrying thoughts. I am loved. I am enough. I am chosen. Remember you are not your anxiety; you feel your anxiety.

_____

_____

_____

_____

_____

_____

_____

Day 28

Gracious words are like a honeycomb,
sweetness to the soul and health to the body.

PROVERBS 16:24 ESV

How do you talk to yourself? Do you use kind words filled with grace? Oftentimes, when I ask people of all ages this question, the quick response is no! My follow-up question is, "Would you speak to someone you love the way you speak to yourself? Would you talk to your parents, siblings, and best friends the way you talk to yourself?"

When you are struggling with anxiety, it can feel really hard to not shame, judge, blame, criticize, and berate yourself. Here's the thing though: just like today's verse says, all the yelling and shaming you do to yourself is only making your anxiety worse. All the self-inflicted yelling and shaming does not make you a better person or create improvement. Change can't happen in shame and judgment because shame and judgment are disconnection. Change and healing only happen in connection—even connection with ourselves. This, my friend, is called self-compassion.

Self-compassion means speaking to yourself the way you would speak to someone you love. When speaking, you choose words that are sweet as honey because they will bring healing to hearts, souls, and bodies.

Think of someone you really care about who is going through a tough time right now. Write a short letter of support to them, just a couple of sentences. Now copy those sentences onto the lines below, address it to yourself, and read it. This is self-compassion. How does it feel?

_____

_____

_____

_____

_____

_____

_____

_____

Day 29

Without counsel, plans go awry,
but in the multitude of counselors they are established.

PROVERBS 15:22 NKJV

Anxiety does a great job of making us believe that we are alone. Our brains often tell us the lies that no one cares, no one will help, we are in this by ourselves, and we can't rely on anyone to help. The Enemy loves using these lies too. Except, we are not alone. Ever. We are not the only ones who have felt this way. We are not the only ones to go through something like this. Even if it's not the exact same situation, someone out there knows how we feel.

Do not let the Enemy or your anxiety tell you otherwise. Reach out. Ask for help. Tell someone what is going on. It is with this counsel, as today's verse says, that connection grows and that we realize we always have community, if only we reach out and allow our community to support us. When we speak our story, we will often be met with a "me too" and "I'm here." We are made for connection and community, we can't do this life on our own, we need each other. Let the people who love and care about you in; let them help.

Who is in your community when it comes to coping with your anxiety?
How do they counsel and/or support you? How could they support
you? When is the last time you asked for support?

_____

_____

_____

_____

_____

_____

_____

_____

_____

_____

_____

_____

_____

_____

_____

_____

Day 30

They help each other and say to their companions, "Be strong!"

ISAIAH 41:6

When we live in community, our anxiety can easily trick us into thinking that we must compare ourselves to others. They are prettier. They are smarter. They are cooler. They seem so put together and don't have to ever worry about anxiety. So often these comparisons only leave us feeling more alone and not okay. In reality, we simply aren't that comparable to one another. No one with your exact genetics, upbringing, and life experiences has ever walked this earth. And no one ever will again.

It is like comparing apples to oranges, and comparison is the thief of our joy and happiness. More than that, for me, it helps to remember that comparison only makes me feel more alone. What if instead of buying into the comparison game, which tears us apart and creates more loneliness than we already feel, we leaned into feeling a little uncomfortable and helped one another. To help one another and say, "Me too! Let's be strong together!"

Do you have someone in your life, perhaps a friend or classmate, that you often compare yourself to? How does that feel? Is it helpful? What if the next time that comparative thought enters your mind, you shift it by asking that friend or classmate how you can support them right now?

_____

_____

_____

_____

_____

_____

_____

_____

_____

_____

_____

_____

Day 31

Set your minds on things above, not on earthly things.

COLOSSIANS 3:2

D o you find this one as difficult as I do? I mean, the things in this world are so shiny and cool. We see over and over how our world prioritizes stuff, titles, and success, whether with money, followers, or likes. And yet, I don't think that when we get to heaven Jesus will ask us how many followers we had. I think He will ask us how well we loved others. Which also means we have to learn how to love ourselves.

One of the things I repeat to myself often—especially when my head, the world, and yes, even anxiety tell me that I need more stuff, more likes, more anything—is that I can't take it with me in the end. To set our minds on things above means to set our minds on heaven. And when I think of heaven I think of a God who created, knows, and loves me. His Son, Jesus, died for me and showed me how to sit beside others and love them well in truth and healing. He showed me that it's people who really matter. I believe if we set our minds on these things, anxiety won't stand a chance.

When you think of things above, what do you think of? How could these things help to shift your anxious thinking?

_____

_____

_____

_____

_____

_____

_____

_____

_____

_____

_____

_____

Day 32

Now to him who is able to do immeasurably more than all we ask or imagine, according to his power that is at work within us.

EPHESIANS 3:20

Accepting Ephesians 3:20 can be hard and even annoying, especially when we feel like we have a whole list of prayers that God hasn't answered. And even more so when anxiety keeps track of all of the prayers we consider unanswered. But God does answer our prayers. Scripture tells us if we ask in His name, He will answer. Here's the tough part: That whole "He is able to do immeasurably more than we ask or imagine" thing often means that the way He answers our prayers is not how or when we want.

Let's not forget the second half of this verse. His power is at work within us. The things we ask and imagine, the things far above and more than what we even think to ask and imagine, are already somehow at work in us through Him. Is it magic? No. At the same time, I have no doubt that when I call Jesus in, when I ask in His name, there is a power that in some way is miraculous . . . dare I say magical. I suppose this is the wonder and awe I wish we didn't allow life, the world, and anxiety to steal from us.

If you allowed yourself to wonder more than what you are asking and imagining in your life from God, what would that look like? Suspending doubt and your anxiety for just a little while today, what would you ask and imagine to be?

_____

_____

_____

_____

_____

_____

_____

_____

_____

_____

_____

_____

_____

Day 33

There is a time for everything,
and a season for every activity under the heavens.

ECCLESIASTES 3:1

In some seasons, everything feels great. You are killing it, you are happy, your anxiety is in check, and everyone is happy with you. Then there are seasons that feel hard, dark, and exhausting. Throughout life, we're taught that things are all good or all bad. We're conditioned to believe that we can only feel one emotion at a time. Not to mention, the basic emotions like happiness, anger, and sadness don't really feel like accurate barometers of emotion. There are a lot of different kinds of happy, mad, and sad. Plus, it is totally possible to feel happy and sad at the same time.

Our brains don't like it because they are wired to keep things simple and safe. When we give ourselves permission to feel more than one emotion at the same time, we honor our full story. This is what I call the permission of The And. To feel more than one thing at the same time, to walk into the messy middle and honor our full truth. If we are honest with ourselves, it is often those tougher seasons that eventually bring us to some of the greatest gifts. That doesn't for one second mean that those tougher seasons don't suck. Because they do. What we can remember, though, is that God is with us. (I know I keep writing this. I just really need you to know it.) Give yourself permission to feel it all through it all.

If you gave yourself permission to feel it all—what I call the permission of The And—what are all the things you are thinking and feeling? Again, remember this is not to make a permanent record; it is simply to get it out, make the dark less powerful, and honor the light.

_____

_____

_____

_____

_____

_____

_____

_____

Day 34

Whatsoever things are true, whatsoever things are honest, whatsoever things are just, whatsoever things are pure, whatsoever things are lovely, whatsoever things are of good report . . . think on these things.

PHILIPPIANS 4:8 KJV

True, honest, just, pure, lovely and good report. Think on these things. That's basically an old-school super-biblical way of saying think on or meditate on the good things of life. This is so much easier said than done, especially when we struggle with anxiety. Anxiety often tells us that if we only focus on the good, we won't be prepared when the not-so-good happens.

Maybe it just feels like there is no room for the good when there is so much anxiety in there. I promise there is room for both. To deny the good or the bad isn't realistic and oftentimes only makes you feel like a fraud—which too often makes us feel even more anxious. When you make room for both, you will know that there is always light in the dark. More than that, our light often only comes out of the dark. Rather than believing you must always think of only the good or meditate on it, choose to make room for the dark and the light. I think then the light will show you that the dark won't last and that the light is more powerful. Because the light is Jesus.

Have you tried meditation? There are so many ways to meditate. We can focus on our breath. We can focus on a verse. Meditation is simply learning how to sit quietly with ourselves. Don't think you have to clear your head or not think at all; that's kind of impossible for most of us. Instead, when a thought comes in, label it as a worry or a to-do or whatever, and then refocus on your breath or the verse. Today, go into a quiet place and meditate. Jot down how it made you feel.

_____

_____

_____

_____

_____

_____

_____

Day 35

I am humbled and quieted in your presence. Like a contented child who rests on its mother's lap, I'm your resting child and my soul is content in you.

PSALM 131:2 TPT

I know we are often taught that God is our Father. A Father without the earthly and human limitations that our earthly fathers have. And yet, there are also places in Scripture where God is referred to as motherly. Whoever is motherly to you, whoever helps take care of you, loves you unconditionally, helps you in many ways, shows you how God loves you too.

Think of when you may have curled up on this person's lap when you were smaller. Maybe she stroked your hair a little or rubbed your back in a constant rhythm and somehow the thing that was so hard and overwhelming became a little less. We can use this same visualization with God or Jesus. In His presence we can and will feel calm. We can quiet ourselves when we choose to feel His presence. Imagine Jesus, whatever you think He looks like. Now imagine that He is sitting on the ground cross-legged, and He invites you to sit beside Him and lean your weight and head on His shoulder or lap. Now just like a mother figure may have done when you were smaller, imagine Jesus taking His hand—yes with the hole in it, the very scar that reminds you of what He did for you—and brushing your hair lightly. The calm. The quiet. The presence. The love.

Breathe. Feel. Receive. How does this image of you and Jesus make you feel?

_____

_____

_____

_____

_____

_____

_____

_____

_____

Day 36

For God has not given us a spirit of fear, but of
power and of love and of a sound mind.

2 TIMOTHY 1:7 NKJV

How can our spirits be of power, love, and a sound
mind when our thoughts are racing, rehearsing, and
worrying? Our bodies are even amped up with racing
hearts, sweaty palms, and gasping breaths. Sometimes,
in this life, our minds and bodies forget the true spirit that
God has put in us. It doesn't mean we are bad, wrong,
or messed up. It simply means we are human in a very
messy world.

Where do you feel your anxiety in your body the
most? Is it racing thoughts, repetitive thoughts, or no
thoughts? Is it a racing heart or a pounding heart? Does
your belly feel yucky? Do your palms sweat? These are
signs that your emotions own you, that right now emotions, maybe especially anxiety, own everything. It is in
these times that it is easy to forget the spirit that God
put in us. It is in these times that our thinking, rational
brain goes off track and too often we hurl our hurt onto

the people we love the most. We yell more, we isolate more, or we check out with things like games, technology, food, exercise, or even schoolwork. Next time you feel your body freaking out with one of those signs, I want you to take a deep breath, get your thinking, rational brain back on track, and remember this affirmation: my spirit, the spirit from God that is full of power, love, and a sound mind, is always in me, no matter how much anxiety tries to distract me from it.

When you think about the spirit that God has given you, what other gifts besides power, love, and a sound mind do you think you have? How can those gifts help you cope with your anxiety today?

_____

_____

_____

_____

_____

_____

_____

Day 37

But those who hope in the LORD will renew their strength.
They will soar on wings like eagles;
they will run and not grow weary,
they will walk and not be faint.

ISAIAH 40:31

It will inevitably happen. You are doing good with staying on track with everything. You are actually doing the things in your self-care routine that help with anxiety. You are feeling good and, dare I say, your anxiety is even a little quiet. Then, *bam*! A test kicks your butt, you get sick, or something difficult happens at home and you fall off track a bit. Then you let your anxiety take that little misstep and turn into a big fat lie that you are already off track, so you might as well just not do any of the things that help. Before you know it, you are hardly doing any of the things that help you cope with your struggles, and anxiety says you can't start over unless you start over with all of it at once.

Just no. Like Isaiah 40:31 says, when we hope in God, our strength will be renewed—it is our permission slip to begin again! Starting over doesn't mean deleting all the progress you've made. It is okay to fall off track. Simply begin again. Begin with one thing that helps you feel not so weary, and run.

Today check in with some of your favorite self-care coping skills. Have you been doing deep breathing exercises? Reading? Listening to music? Praying? Journaling? Which one can you begin again with today?

_____

_____

_____

_____

_____

_____

_____

_____

_____

_____

Day 38

Bad company corrupts good character.

1 CORINTHIANS 15:33

I t's true: the people we spend the most time with have a greater influence on our lives. We must be careful with this mindset (and even a verse like this) because it doesn't mean that we only surround ourselves with people who look like us, think like us, and share the same beliefs. Do not fall into the lie that says different means bad.

How boring would the world be if everyone thought and believed the same things? God made all of His children so different, and He did this for so many reasons. When we surround ourselves with people who don't look like us or have different views, we will find people who complement us, challenge us, and help us grow. Today's verse serves as a reminder. When people pull us out of who God created us to be and away from the gifts of who He is—like grace, kindness, joy, and patience—we must remember that we are not immune to negative influences. Surround yourself with people who help you to be your most authentic self.

Who is in your closest group of friends? Do they know the real you?
Are they a positive influence on you?

_____

_____

_____

_____

_____

_____

_____

_____

_____

_____

_____

_____

Day 39

Do not conform to the pattern of this world, but be transformed by the renewing of your mind.

ROMANS 12:2

Here is that "renew" word again. If only reading the Bible, believing in Jesus, and having faith meant that all the hard stuff was gone. It's easy, especially when anxiety can create so much doubt in us, to think that the ways of this world are easier to get by with.

Let's focus on the word *conform* for a second. Conform means to comply or bend to changing who we are to the things of this world—versus being transformed, which for me means more of a change to the more courageous, healthier versions of who we were meant to be all along. According to Romans 12:2, it comes with some effort—the effort to renew our minds and focus on who God says He is and who we are to Him especially. To renew our minds with Scripture. To renew our minds with awe and wonder. To renew our minds with peace and joy. To renew our minds with the choice to not allow the world to tell us who we should be, rather to live as who

He says we are. Then we can show the world who our Jesus is through and in us.

Be honest with yourself and write down some ways you're conforming to this world. What can do you differently to transform and renew your mind? How will not conforming to those patterns improve your overall well-being?

_____

_____

_____

_____

_____

_____

_____

_____

_____

_____

_____

_____

Day 40

The light shines in the darkness, and the
darkness has not overcome it.

JOHN 1:5 ESV

As I've mentioned before, hardly anything in this life
is all good or all bad; there are often shades of gray,
including the complicated gray. There is always light in
the dark and often our light is born of the dark. When we
know who Jesus is, how He lives in and through us, that
light is more powerful than any darkness that can settle
in and around us. No matter how dark it may feel, light
is always there. This doesn't mean we ooze rainbows and
butterflies or plow through the hard stuff with toxic pos-
itivity. It means that we speak it all, honor our full truth,
and in the darkness trust that somehow and someday it
will be okay.

Actually, it will be better than okay. This is the permission of The And. It's also the promise of God. To give
ourselves permission to feel it all. To walk into the muck
and the mess of the middle, the dark and the light. To say
it sucks and it's hard. To know God is with us, He's got

this (even if we don't understand or like it), and it will be for our good and His glory. As believers we are often told to simply believe, have faith, do not fear, be positive, and never struggle. Except time and again we see Jesus struggle in Scripture. We see His very human experience in struggle alongside the miracle of who He is in God. Because the light is always there.

Write down a hard time when people encouraged you to stay positive and didn't acknowledge how hard something really was. How did their feedback affect you? What light came from your darkness?

_____

_____

_____

_____

_____

_____

_____

_____

Day 41

A cheerful heart is good medicine,
but a crushed spirit dries up the bones.

PROVERBS 17:22

It's typical that when we are cheerful, we feel better. Except sometimes anxiety makes it impossible to be cheerful. What if we shifted how we look at the word cheerful? Other words that we could plug in include joyful, making merry, delighting, or rejoice. I'll admit some of those words—especially when anxiety feels like it has a tight grip on my mind and heart—feel so far away.

Rejoice, for some reason, feels doable. It makes me think of gratitude. I don't mean the kind of gratitude where you use comparison by saying, "At least I have food to eat" or "At least I have shoes that fit my feet." I mean wholehearted gratitude where you can name something you are grateful for even when you're dealing with tough stuff. There are so many ways you can practice gratitude. Research shows us that people who practice daily gratitude are happier, healthier, and, yes, less anxious people.

Here are some ideas of how to practice gratitude:

- Start a group chat with friends or family and every day name something you are grateful for.

- Do a daily gratitude journal and write down three things you are grateful for. The three things need to be different every day so you will appreciate the small things you take for granted. Choose one of those three things and write two to three sentences explaining your gratefulness. Going into the details often deepens the feeling of gratitude.

- Make a list of three things you are grateful for about your personal life (friends, family, hobbies, etc.), then three things about school and/or extracurricular activities, and finally, three things you are grateful for about yourself. Yep, yourself. I know this one may be tough.

Gratitude starts from within. Choose one of these practices today. How did it feel to write it down? The Notes section, in the back of the book, is a great space to create a daily gratitude journal.

Day 42

All things are possible to him who believes.

MARK 9:23 NKJV

All things. Everything. Anything. Is it possible? And all we have to do is believe? When Jesus spoke this to the father of the boy who was tortured by a spirit, could He have also meant it for us today? If only we believe, it is possible? It feels so hard to believe this today even though we read it in red letters in our Bibles. Even though we read Jesus' words in Mark 9 that Jesus healed and freed the boy. Except here we are today, somedays with anxiety so high that it feels hard to go about our normal day, and we are told to believe because if we just believe enough then God will heal us, right?

Except sometimes God takes a really long time to answer that prayer and sometimes the way He answers isn't how we wanted. God is the God who allows really tough things to happen. Yet, He still asks us to turn to Him and believe what His Son said to that father, that all things are possible to those who believe. I've had several things in my life that God chose not to heal, or at least not to heal in the way and time that I wanted and felt I needed. One of the things that has helped me so much, especially in reading all these grand promises in Scripture, is to take them as fact. What if this verse is a simple fact? A fact, not just a belief. What could that mean for you today?

Write down what that fact means to you today.

Day 43

Trust in the LORD with all your heart
and lean not on your own understanding.

PROVERBS 3:5

So much of life, especially when you struggle with anxiety, is about figuring it out. Getting control of something. Fixing it. Making it better. Anxiety says if you can't fix it or fully understand it, then you just have to try harder. Faith says that your understanding will never provide the full understanding because it only comes from trusting God. This doesn't mean a passive faith, where you throw your hands up and stop trying to help yourself or ask for help. It means being confident in God, seeking the support in His Word, His people, and the gifts He put inside of you because there will always be things in your life that are far above and beyond your understanding.

Your brain, which is wired to keep you safe and comfortable, does not like not knowing, or the need for surrender, and anxiety definitely hates the lack of control. In many ways, this trust is the tool to help you move through the uncertainty of it all. When it feels uncertain and anxiety hates everything about that discomfort, you can be secure, with everything you are, in who God says He is and who He says you are. Lean on Him.

Make a list of who God is to you and who God says you are. Even when your anxiety tells you not to believe, this is what you can trust.

_____

_____

_____

_____

_____

_____

_____

_____

_____

_____

_____

_____

Day 44

I do not give to you as the world gives. Do not let your hearts be troubled and do not be afraid.

JOHN 14:27

Our world offers some great gifts—experiences, treasures, and people. However, it is nothing compared to what Jesus gave us and promises us. In John 14 Jesus told His disciples that Holy Spirit was coming to teach and remind them of everything. Let's be honest, it is easy to forget. To know and lean into Holy Spirit is how Jesus gifts us far beyond what the world can promise us or provide. Without Jesus, without His promises and the gifts of Holy Spirit, the things really don't matter much. It is here that we can receive what feels like an impossible feat of not being afraid or troubled.

I wonder if when Jesus said not to let our hearts be troubled and not to be afraid, he also meant, "Hey, I know you will feel trouble and fear. Feel it and do not be it." There is a difference between feeling our emotions and being our emotions. We are not mad. We feel mad. When we attach to our feelings, we often identify with them, making it far too easy to forget who we really are.

When you feel your emotions, speak them correctly, and cope with them in a healthy way, your emotions won't own your story; they will simply be passing energies that make life a little more interesting.

Today, if your anxiety amps up, try saying, "I am feeling anxiety" rather than "I am anxious." How does that feel different? How will feeling your emotions versus being your emotions help you?

_____

_____

_____

_____

_____

_____

_____

_____

_____

Day 45

Do to others what you would have them do to you.

MATTHEW 7:12

T he Golden Rule we are all taught is to treat others the way we would like to be treated. All good and fine, especially, I think, when it comes to what Jesus was referring to, which was to extend grace, generosity, love, and kindness to all people. When we remember that every human we meet is created in God's image, and is therefore a reflection of our loving Creator, it feels easier to meet them with grace, love, and kindness, even if they don't meet us with the same. This is who Jesus is and who He tells us to be. However, the Golden Rule is best applied when we remember to add empathy to it. We are all very different and what you want in a relationship (or an interaction) may be different from what someone else wants.

Empathy is to meet someone with the presence of who Jesus is and identify with what they may be feeling. Empathy is to sit beside someone and seek to understand them. Not necessarily agree with them, simply to seek to understand what their life is like. When we choose empathy while also living out today's verse, I think we will find that our relationships are better, we appreciate more people (even those who are different from us), and kindness wins.

What do you think of the Golden Rule? When was the last time you chose to seek to understand someone who believed something different from you with kindness and grace? What was that like? How did this change your perspective of this person or a topic?

_____

_____

_____

_____

_____

_____

_____

_____

_____

Day 46

You can't keep your true self hidden forever;
before long you'll be exposed.

LUKE 12:2 MSG

When we feel like we aren't doing well or we are struggling, the last person we want to turn to is the first person we need. Maybe we don't turn to God because we are mad at Him or because we think He would be disappointed in us. Maybe we are believing the lies our anxiety (or religion) tells us that He is the unfair and punishing God. So, we don't pray. We don't pause and ask Him for help. We don't talk to Him.

I promise you, He can handle it. He can handle our big, huge, and not-so-fun emotions. He is big enough to take it. Even if you want to yell and tell Him you are mad and that this feels so unfair, He can take it. And more than that, He already knows. He already knows how you feel and He loves you all the same. The more we hide from God, the more it usually means that He will continue to refine us until we have no choice but to finally turn it over to Him. So, begin with turning to Him and talking. Yell if you must. Tell Him you are doubting His goodness. Ask for what you want and need, and then listen. More than that, know He hears you, He knows, and He is with you.

When is the last time you let God know you were mad or frustrated with Him? What stops you from turning to Him?

_____

_____

_____

_____

_____

_____

_____

_____

_____

_____

_____

Day 47

The unfolding of your words gives light;
it gives understanding to the simple.

PSALM 119:130

I know we are supposed to read His Word every day. We are supposed to commit it to memory. We are supposed to renew our minds with it. We are supposed to be His living example of it. Yet some days, it just feels hard to do. Some days I forget. Then before I know it it's been a week or more since I've opened my Bible. I also know that if I am praying and talking to God throughout my days, reading some devotionals, and listening to worship music, this can be enough during some seasons of life. God never told us that we had to do this faithful life perfectly.

What I love about Psalm 119:130 is the word unfolding. It also means opening. When we open His Word, we will have light and understanding in our lives. When we make space to receive His Word, His plan can feel like it unfolds so we can have a better understanding.

Did you notice that the verse says His Word will give understanding to the simple? If that is in Scripture, can you imagine what His Word will do for us when things feel complicated? Like our anxiety.

Today, read an extra Scripture. Maybe it is today's verse plus the verses just before and just after it. Unfold a little extra today and receive the light and understanding that God has for you. Write down which additional Scripture you decided to read. Do you have any additional takeaways?

_____

_____

_____

_____

_____

_____

_____

_____

_____

_____

Day 48

Faith is the substance of things hoped for,
the evidence of things not seen.

HEBREWS 11:1 KJV

There are things you can't see, and still you know they exist. This is faith. In Hebrews 11:1, we see the word *substance*, which kind of feels incompatible. Substance seems tangible, something we can feel with our hands, see with our eyes, and yet the verse goes on to say "evidence of things not seen."

How can you see faith? What does faith look like and feel like to you? For me faith is in feeling my anxiety, still doing the things that I know will help and move me through it and forward in my journey of healing. Faith is in the practice of reading Scripture, listening to worship music, making time to connect with friends and family, and spending time in nature and awe every day. For me, these are the tangible practices of faith. They help me believe in the things I can't necessarily put my fingers on, like grace, kindness, patience, joy, and love. If we really think about it, our everyday actions are actually ways these gifts become tangible, seen and felt—even if our anxiety sometimes tells us otherwise.

Write down some of the everyday things that make your faith tangible.

_____

_____

_____

_____

_____

_____

_____

_____

_____

_____

_____

_____

_____

Day 49

"Slow down. Take a deep breath. What's the hurry?
Why wear yourself out? Just what are you after anyway?"

JEREMIAH 2:25 MSG

Do more. Try harder. Do better. Maybe these are some of the things your anxiety tells you. Except, what I have learned over and over, despite what my anxiety tells me will work and what the world expects of me, is that rest is the answer. You are more than what you produce. You are more than your grades. You are more than what you will put on your college applications. In many ways, we cannot outdo anxiety. When was the last time you paused, rested, restored, refilled, and took a deep breath? I know it is hard to pause because our brains and the world often tell us to do more, try harder, and do better.

If we keep going, if we keep plowing through, if we keep trying to give from our tired, empty, and burnt-out selves, we will eventually wear out and crash. Pausing when we are overwhelmed means getting our bearings. Resting when we have so much to do refills our energy and resets our mindset, so we can get everything done.

Taking a deep breath, when we want to react, will bring life and help us respond in a more courageous way.

Look at your schedule for today. Schedule short breaks—three-, five-, or ten-minute breaks—so you can slow down, pause, rest, and breathe. Set a timer if you need to. At the end of the day, write about how it felt during and after.

_____

_____

_____

_____

_____

_____

_____

_____

_____

_____

Day 50

For as he thinks in his heart, so is he.

PROVERBS 23:7 NKJV

It is true that our thoughts greatly influence how we feel and behave. Some psychology theories say if you can change the way you think, you will change the way you feel, and then you can change your behavior. Sometimes it feels linear and even simple. If I capture my anxious thinking, challenge it, and rewrite it, my feelings will follow suit and change. Which then means my behaviors are more easily changed too. But the reality is, it isn't always linear.

When we are living in a courageous and more wholehearted way, we want to be more integrated. Which means our thoughts, feelings, and behaviors are connected and help us move through our anxiety. For example, think of the last time you were feeling anxious. What did you feel in your body? What was your thinking? What was your behavior? Maybe you felt your heart racing and your head was shouting, "I am totally anxious, oh crap!" And so you did that thing that you think calms your anxiety, such as biting your nails, rewriting your list for the fifth time, or checking your bookbag again. Except that behavior reinforces the anxious thinking, which then tells your body, which then makes your heart beat even faster. What if you named the anxious feeling with something like, "this is my anxious brain"? Then ask yourself two questions: What concrete evidence do I have to support the need to feel anxious? Can I feel this and cope with it in a healthy way and allow it to pass?

This is integrating it all and choosing to feel your anxiety and not be your anxiety.

Write down some of the healthy ways you can cope with your anxiety.

_____

_____

_____

_____

_____

_____

_____

Day 51

> But small is the gate and narrow the road that
> leads to life, and only a few find it.

MATTHEW 7:14

Always remember that small and narrow doesn't mean perfect. We don't have to be perfect to have life with Jesus. We don't have to be perfect to get over our anxiety. Perfectionism isn't possible, even though our anxiety leads us to believe otherwise.

Perfectionism sets us up for failure. When I try to do and say and be everything perfectly, I set myself up for failure. And then I believe the lie that anxiety and perfectionism tell me that I have to be even more perfect next time, rather than acknowledge the truth that perfectionism isn't possible. Life with God is a journey. Sure, we have an incredible destination. Eternity with Jesus sounds pretty amazing. However, if we believe we must be perfect to get there, we aren't accepting the invitation that Jesus gave us when He died for us. The invitation to live life now with God.

Perfectionism makes us believe that we can't reach

our destination or even have God with us during the journey, unless we do it all perfectly. However, if we did everything perfect, we would never have an opportunity to learn and grow.

I don't know about you, but I haven't learned from the hilltops; I have learned my best lessons from the valleys. When I am down and out and asking Jesus for help, it is then He does His best work. It is then He shows me that road to life, the life with Him.

Do you consider yourself to be a perfectionist? Are you willing to challenge that part of your anxiety? Make a list of the things you need to let go. Beside each item, write down how you can let go of perfectionism.

_____

_____

_____

_____

_____

_____

_____

Day 52

Be patient and stand firm.

JAMES 5:8

P atience is something I am constantly working on. I am simply not a patient person. I've prayed and reminded God that He made me this way and yet He keeps asking me to be patient and wait. I walk fast. I do everything fast. Which means I break a lot of stuff and redo things often because I rush through it the first time. Patience is a lesson the Lord is constantly teaching me. I've also learned that standing firm means to be resolute in my beliefs, in my knowing that God is here, and that Jesus is coming. Living life with those beliefs requires patience!

In James 5:7, the farmer waits for the land to yield valuable crops. Of course, waiting happens after the work of prepping the soil, planting the seeds, and trusting that God will provide the nourishment of the sun and rain. In life, we have limited control. Like the farmer, we do the work of planting and tending the soil. Then we must wait and see how God provides, standing firm that He will show up and the harvest will come.

What have you worked hard on, taken care of, and had to wait until God provided? What helped you patiently wait?

_____

_____

_____

_____

_____

_____

_____

_____

_____

_____

_____

_____

_____

Day 53

Don't worry or surrender to your fear. For you've believed in God, now trust and believe in me also.

JOHN 14:1 TPT

I love how Jesus told his disciples to surrender their fear. He was basically saying, feel the fear and trust anyway.

We can't be fearless. We are human beings with emotions and full lives in a wild world. Realistically, being fearless wouldn't be very safe or smart. We have our fears and our anxieties to keep us safe. However, it is when those fears and anxieties take over our lives, change who we are, and stop us from walking in God's truth and in who He created us to be that our fears and anxieties no longer keep us safe, rather they hold us back.

Jesus was living, breathing, and eating in front of them and the disciples still struggled to believe. I think it is helpful to remember this when our fears and anxieties tell us we have to be fearless and have faith because Jesus said so. Maybe it just isn't that simple. Jesus was man and is God. This is the mystery of our faith. Choosing to trust and believe in who Jesus said He was are the actions we take to walk out our faith.

What fears and anxieties have turned unhealthy for you? Remember, when you identify these things it can be easier to spot them, challenge them, and turn them around before your anxiety continues to grow.

_____

_____

_____

_____

_____

_____

_____

_____

_____

_____

_____

_____

_____

_____

_____

Day 54

We know that God causes all things to work together for good to those who love God, to those who are called according to His purpose.

ROMANS 8:28 NASB

When you choose to love God, you can be sure that He will work everything out for your good. Even when things aren't good. Even when it is dark. Even when your anxiety feels like it is pulling you into a shadowy hole and you're struggling to catch your breath. God has a plan, even when it doesn't seem like His plan is awesome or fun.

I don't think God ever said we can't be nervous or question His plan. Alongside doubt is our faith and surrendered trust that He will use it for our good. Sometimes I find it helpful to remember that God is weaving together a masterpiece tapestry with millions of threads, colors, and textures. Except I don't get to see the pretty side of it; only He and all of eternity does. We get to see the loose ends, the knots, the messiness underneath the tapestry that looks like a hot mess. We are part of His masterpiece, His plan, and we can trust the beauty and the good of it, even though it's hard to see and feel many days.

Sometimes keeping a list of God's blessings, answered prayers, and how He showed up in tough seasons helps us remember His faithfulness in dark times. Today make a list of some of the toughest seasons you've been through, and then include all of the miracles and the presence of God that you felt and saw through those seasons. Add the answered prayers to this list too. If you need help getting started, think of things you have now that you wouldn't have had without those tough times.

_____

_____

_____

_____

_____

_____

_____

_____

_____

_____

Day 55

There is no room in love for fear. Well-formed love banishes
fear. Since fear is crippling, a fearful life—fear of death,
fear of judgment—is one not yet fully formed in love.

1 JOHN 4:18 MSG

Initially, when reading today's verse, I cringed because,
honestly, it contradicts what I experience every day and
what I teach—which is why I recommend taking a deeper
look beyond the original language. I do believe that we
can feel fear and love at the same time. This doesn't mean
that love should be fearful or feel chaotic or unsafe.

The love referenced here is agape love. It is the love
that is perfect because it is the love that Jesus loves us
with. It is also the kind of love He asks us to love Him and
others with. In other translations of this verse it actually
says "perfect love," and we know how I feel about the
word perfect. Since we can't be perfect, and only Jesus is
without sin and therefore perfect, are we bound to always
have fear in our lives? I don't think so.

What if we lived our lives knowing that we are loved
by a perfect love in that He sacrificed everything for us.

Fear can't stand up to this kind of love. Since we have this love inside of us, there is no room for fear. When we live from this love, it is easier to remember that fear is just a feeling and not who we are.

Do you think fear and love can be felt at the same time? What is it like? When you remember that Jesus loves us with a divine and sacrificial love, how does that feel?

_____

_____

_____

_____

_____

_____

_____

_____

_____

Day 56

Speaking the truth with love, we will grow up in every way into Christ, who is the head.

EPHESIANS 4:15 NCV

There is a big difference between telling people about Jesus with love versus casting judgment and implying they are wrong. When we are confident in our faith we may come across as unkind, judgmental, and arrogant, which is not a way to show someone Jesus. It is also not what today's verse says will help us become more like Jesus.

Jesus didn't cast judgment toward people who were different from Him and His disciples. Even when He let people know that they weren't living their best life, in alignment with God, He didn't do it standing above them, pointing His finger and shouting at them. Instead, He sat beside them and talked with them about who they really were in and through God. When we love people with truth, which means loving them with grace and kindness, they will meet Jesus through us. And when we love people like Jesus did, we become more like Him.

When was the last time you tried to share your faith with someone?
Do you think you came across as loving? Why or why not? How can you
share your faith with more grace and love, like Jesus, next time?

_____

_____

_____

_____

_____

_____

_____

_____

_____

_____

_____

_____

_____

Day 57

Whoever does not love does not know God, because God is love.

1 JOHN 4:8 NCV

Our brains are wired for comfort and safety. They are also wired for story. This means, oftentimes, it's much easier to live from the stories we make up about others, especially the really judgmental stories. Our brains like to keep it simple, and judging others feels simple and sometimes even safe. When I make up a story about someone, I can adjust how I act around that person, which makes me believe that I am safer.

When judgment and anxiety are writing the stories, things become even more complicated. The stories aren't usually based on concrete evidence; they are created from assumptions, past grievances, and often have more to do with us than the individual we are judging. This isn't Christlike, it isn't loving, it isn't of God. The next time your brain starts making up stories about someone, try pausing, taking a deep breath to get your thinking brain back on track, and ask yourself a few questions: What are the stories really about? What is this bringing up for me?

Do I have evidence to support this story I am making up? And then seek to know more about that person from a place of loving curiosity. Be like Jesus!

Can you think of a time when your mind created a story derived from judgment and preconceived notions? If you had stopped your mind from creating this story, how would the situation have changed? How would your relationship with that person be different?

_____

_____

_____

_____

_____

_____

_____

_____

_____

_____

Day 58

> What you say can mean life or death. Those who speak with care will be rewarded.
>
> PROVERBS 18:21 NCV

Words are powerful. If we believe the Word of God, we know that the tongue can bring life or death. If we listen to our parental figures, we know that certain words aren't allowed in our homes. If we listen to therapists, we know that our language can change everything. We've talked already about attaching to our emotions (remember, I *feel* anxious, and not, I *am* anxious). The words we choose to put after *I am* are very powerful. They are the difference between hard days and brighter days. They can fuel our anxiety, or they can help us cope with our anxiety. We have also talked about self-compassion and how to talk to ourselves the way we'd talk to someone we love.

Another shift in language that has helped me is to name what I am struggling with. How often do we say something like, "I'm bad at _____." I am sure you've even heard adults in your life say it. Today I want you to shift that language to, "I struggle with _____." Then if you want to take it even further, end it with, "I am doing _____ to improve." When we shift our language, we empower ourselves to make changes that move us forward in our healing.

What is the last thing you said you were bad at? Rewrite that into an "I struggle with" statement followed by what you are learning and doing to improve.

I struggle with _____.

I am doing _____ to improve.

Day 59

Knowledge puffs you up with pride, but love builds up.

1 CORINTHIANS 8:1 NCV

When knowledge puffs us up, it can make us unapproachable and arrogant. Our pride can make it difficult for those we care about to show up as their full and whole selves, flaws and all, with us. Sometimes this results from our having strong opinions and coming across as close-minded to other ways of thinking. Sometimes those strong beliefs can even become idols that we begin to put above everything else, including God. When this happens it's easy to believe that it is us versus them, or group others into being right or wrong. Except we don't want to be like the Pharisees and put the rules, the doctrine, or knowledge above God's people. We can love people and still hold true to our values and opinions.

It is possible to disagree with someone and still love them well, and even be friends. Judgment—telling someone they are wrong, shaming them, and trying to convince them to think like us—is not about love; it's usually about being right. Seeking to understand why they think the way they think in curiosity and choosing empathy is loving. It builds a bridge between two children of the King, and it is that bridge that helps them see Jesus in us.

Have you lost a friendship to judgment or difference of opinion? Do you think curiosity could have helped the friendship? Do you have friends in your life who believe differently than you? How can you build them up and love them well?

_____

_____

_____

_____

_____

_____

_____

_____

_____

_____

Day 60

As God's chosen people, holy and dearly loved, clothe yourselves with compassion, kindness, humility, gentleness and patience.

COLOSSIANS 3:12

God chose you. You are therefore holy and dearly loved. Your brain may kind of freak out with those words, especially if anxiety is beating down the door today. What does "holy and dearly loved" mean?

In this verse, holy means set apart by (or for) God. Special. Known. Chosen. Sacred to Him. So loved that He died for you. We must settle into the first part of this verse and receive this love and identity. We are chosen by God and dearly loved, so we must clothe ourselves with or put on these characteristics that Jesus showed us over and over in the gospels. To have compassion means to show mercy, grace, and love to those who are suffering because we are all connected, all children of God, and all in this together.

Kindness can be a tenderness in action and empathy helps bring compassion to life. Humility is to stay grounded and the willingness to approach things with curiosity and never claim to be the expert of anyone else's life except our own. We can do all of this with gentleness, which means we must have patience to keep going, to keep trying, and to keep loving one another like Jesus.

Have you ever considered yourself to be chosen, holy, and dearly loved? How does it feel? How can you show this kind of love to others?

_____

_____

_____

_____

_____

_____

_____

_____

_____

_____

Day 61

Grace and peace be given to you more and more,
because you truly know God and Jesus our Lord.

2 PETER 1:2 NCV

When we live in relationship with God, we are never finished learning about who He is, especially as our faith grows and changes. As we grow and change, our relationship with God and Jesus will too. There will be seasons where we feel so close to Them. There will be seasons where They feel so far away. There will be seasons when we are far away from Them. And then everything in between. We are still in relationship with Them though, we still learn about Them throughout, which means we are always knowing Them more and differently every day.

This verse promises you that when you choose to live in and through this relationship, even during the tough seasons, you will have grace and peace more and more. This means abundance multiplied. I don't know about you, but grace and peace are things I always need. God is your grace and peace. You feel more grace and peace because of and through Him. These gifts of His also live in you. Receive them!

What does grace mean to you? How do you live in grace? What does
peace mean to you? How do you live in peace?

_____

_____

_____

_____

_____

_____

_____

_____

_____

_____

_____

_____

_____

Day 62

This is my command—be strong and courageous! Do not be afraid or discouraged. For the LORD your God is with you wherever you go.

JOSHUA 1:9 NLT

I love the command in today's verse because it feels assertive, confident, and true. You can *feel* afraid, and you don't have to *be* afraid. People who are strong and courageous feel their feelings, speak them, cope with them in a healthy way, and refuse to *be* them!

I must admit, there have been darker than dark times in my life when I have told God that I didn't feel like His presence was enough. So, I asked Him to show up in a way that I would not mistake as chance—a way that I would know was Him. Choosing to ask God for this and to believe in Him is also courageous. This is your faith speaking and leaning into vulnerability because it feels risky and uncertain. Will God show up? He will always show up because He is always with you. You must make sure that you are doing the work to keep your eyes and heart open enough to feel and see Him. For me this means making sure I rest, write, read His Word, listen to worship music, move my body, do breathing exercises, and other self-care things every day. These actions help me live courageously, *feel* my fear rather than *be* my fear, and give me the ability to see and feel God more.

Have you ever felt like you needed more than God's presence in your life? Have you told Him that? Have you ever asked Him to show you His presence? How did He show up?

_____

_____

_____

_____

_____

_____

_____

_____

_____

_____

Day 63

You who are younger, submit yourselves to your elders. All of you, clothe yourselves with humility toward one another, because, "God opposes the proud but shows favor to the humble."

1 PETER 5:5

It is important to have people in our lives who are older, more experienced, and wiser because it provides us with opportunities to learn and grow. Seeking wisdom from our elders will help us learn from their triumphs and falls, and offer an insightful perspective on what we could be overlooking.

God doesn't want us to be prideful or arrogant. He wants us to be humble, curious, and choose to love others. I am not saying that God—or the world, for that matter— makes this task easy. It can feel hard to love someone well and stay curious about them when we know we have very different beliefs about something, especially when that something is very important to us. Remember, it's not our job to convince someone or to alter their stance—that's pride. Our job is to show them who Jesus is through grace and love.

Who are the elders or older people that you look up to? Why do you consider them to be wise? When was the last time you spent time with them or spoke to them? What can you (or have you) learned from them?

_____

_____

_____

_____

_____

_____

_____

_____

_____

_____

_____

_____

Day 64

Be diligent to be found by Him in peace,
without spot and blameless.

2 PETER 3:14 NKJV

I have to be careful with how my anxiety and especially my perfectionism reads today's verse. It is easy to get tripped up on the words and believe that I must be pure and perfect to have peace with Jesus. Except Jesus was the one without sin, not us. He was perfect. Not us.

It is through grace—not our works—and faith that we are made right in His eyes. We must be diligent about this faith because the world will do everything it can to make us doubt it. Diligence may look like breath prayers, journaling, reading Scripture, attending worship services, listening to worship music, or serving. These things can help us see and feel Jesus in the world; they are not things we check off to be good enough for Jesus to love us.

Your faith is not a checklist or even rules that you must follow. Your faith is a messy journey where you believe (and yes, sometimes even question) that you were created by a loving God, who loved you enough to come to earth as a man and die for you because you are His beloved child.

What does diligence look like for you in your faith? Have you tried to be good enough for Jesus? Today, how can you choose to receive His love and grace rather than earn it?

_____

_____

_____

_____

_____

_____

_____

_____

_____

_____

_____

Day 65

God met me more than halfway,
he freed me from my anxious fears.

PSALM 34:4 MSG

You've read it over and over in Scripture. You've read it throughout this book. God is here. God is with you. Always. THE MESSAGE translation of Psalm 34:4 creates a beautiful image. God meets you more than halfway because He is with you. Waiting for you to turn to Him, waiting for you to speak, waiting for you to take His hand so He can show you the way.

You'll feel a sense of freedom when you allow God to see the real you because you'll be met with His perfect love. That perfect love where fear cannot live and you do not have to *be* your fear. You can *feel* your fear, name it, and then tell it, "I'm going to turn my back on you and take a step toward my loving Father. He is behind me, beside me, in front of me, and in me, and already waiting for me more than halfway with His perfect grace and love. Fear, you aren't welcome here."

What is fear telling you today? Can you *feel* it, turn your back to it, and face God, who is waiting to meet you more than halfway? What do you think God is saying to you?

_____

_____

_____

_____

_____

_____

_____

_____

_____

_____

_____

_____

_____

_____

Day 66

Now may our Lord Jesus Christ himself and God our Father, who loved us and by his grace gave us eternal comfort and a wonderful hope, comfort you and strengthen you in every good thing you do and say.

2 THESSALONIANS 2:16–17 NLT

Identifying who the three parts of the Trinity are has allowed me to deepen my faith and my relationship with God. I identify God as our Creator, the Father figure, and the all-powerful loving part. Jesus is an empathic friend, the healer, the miracle worker, the part that oozes love, grace, mercy, and even emotion. And Holy Spirit the creative, joy-filled, fun, breath, that leads and feels, and always shows up for me.

When I read 2 Thessalonians 2:16–17, I marvel at the phrases "eternal comfort" and "wonderful hope." A comfort that is forever, far beyond our lives here and beyond our understanding, alongside the wonderful hope that sounds too good to be true. Then the verse rounds out with saying we will be strengthened in every good thing we say and do through that love and grace, comfort and hope. It all sounds too magical to be real. Nevertheless, when I remind myself of who God and Jesus are to me, I see the magic become the truth.

Who is God to you? Who is Jesus to you? How do their characteristics bring truth to eternal comfort, wonderful hope, and strength?

_____

_____

_____

_____

_____

_____

_____

_____

_____

_____

Day 67

The LORD your God is with you, the Mighty Warrior who saves.
He will take great delight in you; in his love he will no longer
rebuke you, but will rejoice over you with singing.

ZEPHANIAH 3:17

A Mighty Warrior who also delights in us might seem counterintuitive or a bit off. When I picture God as the Mighty Warrior He is, the Warrior who saves me, I see Him fighting on my behalf. I also see Him providing protection for me and being my shelter. This power keeps me safe. This Mighty Warrior, all-powerful God, also delights in us. He cheers for us. He is interested in everything about us and rejoices over us. If we take it even further and remember that His Son, Jesus, died for us and therefore lives in us, He sees not only His beloved child in us, He also sees His Son.

That is a delighting Father. A Father who can unconditionally love. A Father who always shows up. A Father who fights for us and beside us. The verse even goes so far as to say that God rejoices over us with singing. It sounds kind of ridiculous and a bit mind-blowing. And what I love most is that it shatters anxiety's lie. The lie that says I can't approach God because He is mean, unfair, and punishing. I will hold on to the picture of a happy Warrior God who is full of song and is fighting for me.

How does it feel to know that God is a Mighty Warrior fighting on your behalf? What picture do you see when you read that the Mighty Warrior is a rejoiceful singer?

_____

_____

_____

_____

_____

_____

_____

_____

_____

_____

Day 68

I am the LORD your God, who holds your right hand,
and I tell you. "Don't be afraid. I will help you."

ISAIAH 41:13 NCV

Remember when you were little and an adult would hold your hand when crossing the street? They would look down at you and say, "What do we do when crossing the street or walking in a parking lot?" You'd parrot what they had told you over and over in your little kid voice: "We grab an adult's hand and look both ways." I think that universal advice is the world's version of Isaiah 41:13.

In everything you experience, work through, and survive, God wants you to remember to take His hand. In fact, when you forget to take His hand, He will still hold yours and lead the way forward. Then He leans down, takes your face in His hands, looks you in the eyes, and tells you, "Don't be afraid. I will help you. I will guide you. I will show you the way. I will never leave you. I won't forsake you either. I am here. It is good and if it isn't good right now, it will be. I won't let go of your hand. I promise it will get better. Do not be afraid, I'm here."

Is there something you are going through right now that you haven't grabbed God's hand through? What's it like to know He has your hand right now and that He is helping you?

_____

_____

_____

_____

_____

_____

_____

_____

_____

_____

_____

_____

_____

_____

Day 69

Don't lose your bold, courageous faith, for
you are destined for a great reward!

HEBREWS 10:35 TPT

Life isn't as tough when we hold on to our bold and courageous faith. We aren't in this alone because God has a plan. Sometimes it is easy to forget this, but our bold and courageous faith means we are destined for a great reward. There will be great eternal reward when we meet Jesus in heaven. The rewards on earth are fun and shiny and the world values them so much; it is hard not to want more of the shiny things. Trophies, money, shoes, trendy clothes, more followers, and more likes. Except those rewards are bleak in comparison to the rewards we will receive in heaven. The heavenly rewards come from our powerful faith, and sharing that faith with others. By using grace, kindness, and love in our relationships, we are showing people who Jesus is. Community may not seem as fancy as stuff; however, I have no doubt it is what Jesus meant when He told us to love His people.

How do you show the world your bold and courageous faith? What do
you think eternal reward means? What are some ways you can live out
your faith in a bolder and more courageous way?

_____

_____

_____

_____

_____

_____

_____

_____

_____

_____

_____

_____

_____

Day 70

In all the work you are doing, work the best you can. Work as if you were doing it for the Lord, not for people.

COLOSSIANS 3:23 NCV

Doing your best doesn't mean that you'll always get it right. Doing your best means you give all that you have. It means asking for help when you need it and saying "I don't know" when you're not sure. Doing your best means showing up as your full self, flaws and all. Doing your best means showing the world who Jesus is because you live for God.

It is important, especially when you struggle with anxiety, to know that everyone else is also doing their best. In any given moment of your life, even when you are messing something up, it is your best. If you would've known better, you would have chosen better. This doesn't mean you can't grow, learn, and change. In that moment though, it was your best, it's what you had. Accepting and understanding this is part of extending grace and generosity to yourself and to others. Giving grace to ourselves and others, knowing that everyone is doing their best, and doing it all for the Lord is the perfect way to show people who Jesus is.

Do you believe you are doing your best? What would it feel like to live and know that you are doing your best? How do you extend grace to others? Write down ways you could extend more grace to people.

_____

_____

_____

_____

_____

_____

_____

_____

_____

_____

Day 71

In the same way, let your light shine before others, that they may see your good deeds and glorify your Father in heaven.

MATTHEW 5:16

Here's another way to read today's verse: let your radiance give light. Sometimes the world can feel like a super-dark place. There is so much going on. With all of the uncertainty and division in the world, your mind might wonder what exactly God's plan is. Or even where He is.

Think of how much could be shifted if we simply showed the world who we are in Jesus. To leave them in awe of the light we shine. To leave them thinking, I don't know what they have, I just know I want more of it. When we exude the gifts of God, people will feel drawn to us and they will feel God. This is what it means to let our light shine before others; it is to shine the love and grace of Jesus to the world. Sure, this is through good deeds such as treating people with kindness, serving, leading, showing the world our talents, and giving glory to God through it all. However, it is also through our presence of being with other people. Glorifying God doesn't have to mean that we are talking about Him all the time or reciting Scripture to everyone. It can be as simple as sitting beside people and loving them well.

How do you shine your light into the world? How can you let your radiance give light today?

_____

_____

_____

_____

_____

_____

_____

_____

_____

_____

_____

Day 72

The Lord will work out his plans for my life—
for your faithful love, O Lord, endures forever.
Don't abandon me, for you made me.

PSALM 138:8 NLT

God will work it out for good. It would be nice to know when this is happening and the exact plan of action, right?

Faith doesn't work that way. We do know that He has a plan for everything. He has a plan when things are going great. He has a plan when things aren't going so great and we want to question His plan. Other translations of today's verse read that God will perfect that which concerns us.

All the things I am hoping for, working toward, and yes, even wishing for matter to God. They matter to Him and He is working on them, even when I can't see it or feel it. His faithfulness and love endure all things. They work higher than we can ever comprehend and we can trust that He will not turn His back on us. He has a plan. We are part of that plan. He will make good on it. We must hold on and keep going.

What concerns are you hoping God will perfect? How can you see
God's plan and your plan coming together?

_____

_____

_____

_____

_____

_____

_____

_____

_____

_____

_____

_____

_____

_____

_____

Day 73

Don't be afraid, for I am with you.
Don't be discouraged, for I am your God.
I will strengthen you and help you.
I will hold you up with my victorious right hand.

ISAIAH 41:10 NLT

When Scripture is written like this, like a letter or even a bit of a loving lecture from Father God, I find it helpful. The words are clear and kindly communicate exactly what He wants from us and the reason why we can trust it. He's very clear. "Don't be afraid because I am with you. And always am, right beside and in. Don't be discouraged because I am your God. I've got this." Then He finishes the loving lecture with some additional promises. "You are strong through Me. I am helping you. You can stand up, I've got you."

I think it is easy to feel like we are in the ocean and can't quite get our bearings in the waves. We may even lose our balance and end up with sand in our suit. Sometimes if it gets really bad, we forget which way is up and saltwater gets up our nose. We struggle and wear ourselves out trying to save ourselves, when sometimes all we need to remember is that the water isn't that deep, and we need to stand up. We can stand on the foundation of who God is and what He promises. Stand up, brush the sand off, snort the salt-water out, and walk on the foundation you can trust.

When was a time you found yourself struggling, like in the waves, and you needed a reminder to just stand on the foundation of who God is and His promises? What are some things you could do today to remind yourself of His foundation?

_____

_____

_____

_____

_____

_____

_____

_____

_____

_____

Day 74

I've learned by now to be quite content whatever my circumstances. I'm just as happy with little as with much, with much as with little.

PHILIPPIANS 4:11 MSG

It can be tough not to want more. To want more cool shoes, to be involved in more sports, to want more books, to want more time, to want more energy, to want more money, more happiness, more stuff, or more of basically anything. We are told over and over in Scripture that all we need is Jesus. In Philippians 4:11, we read that we can learn to be content with little and with much. When we find our peace in who Jesus is, no matter how much we have, we have enough. He is enough. We are enough. Just enough.

Here's what I really need you to hear though. You are enough. Just enough. You don't have to earn it or strive for it. You were created by an all-loving God and you are loved so much that He sacrificed His only Son for you. Jesus loves you so much He suffered and died for you. We didn't deserve it—this is grace. However, this does not mean we are unworthy of it. There's a difference. We may not deserve the loving grace that Jesus gave us.

Yet He gives it to us anyway because we are worth that much to Him. That's enough. He's enough. You are too!

Be honest and fill in the blank. Never _____ enough. What does your head and the world fill that blank in with? Pretty enough? Rich enough? Good enough? Smart enough?

Now write down what it would feel like to know and live like you are enough?

_____

_____

_____

Fill in the blank and use these as daily affirmations.

I am _____ enough.

I am _____ enough.

I am _____ enough.

I am _____ enough.

I am _____ enough.

I am _____ enough.

Day 75

Stand firm then, with the belt of truth buckled around your waist, with the breastplate of righteousness in place, and with your feet fitted with the readiness that comes from the gospel of peace.

EPHESIANS 6:14-15

T his is the kind of armor we must live with. Not the armor of hustling for our enoughness. Not the armor of perfectionism, worrying, striving, earning, or people-pleasing. That armor only hides our true selves. That armor doesn't show the world who we really are, which also means the world can't see Jesus in and through us.

We must remember and know we are standing in the armor of God because it helps us live from the truth of grace and love. This armor also protects us and helps us fight the flaming arrows of the Evil One. This protection is equipped with the tools we need to challenge our anxious thinking, to counter the unhealthy messages of the world, to stand in the truth that we are loved, and that we have peace living in us.

Recite Ephesians 6:14–15 out loud while standing in the truth of who Jesus is. While you're reading out loud, envision or motion with your hands putting on the armor of God. What does that feel like? Do you feel more confident? What does the armor help you overcome or tackle?

_____

_____

_____

_____

_____

_____

_____

_____

_____

_____

_____

_____

Day 76

The peace of God, which surpasses all comprehension,
will guard your hearts and your minds in Christ Jesus.

PHILIPPIANS 4:7 NASB

Some days it can feel like everything is all over the place, the world is a mess, and life is just hard. We see the pain around us, maybe even feel it in us, and still there is this voice inside us reassuringly saying it will be okay. Some days that voice is super tiny and doesn't feel as powerful as the darkness in the world. Some days that voice is roaring throughout and through us. It's a voice that can feel silly or even not enough, and yet we must hold on to it. This is the peace of God and like today's verse says, it isn't supposed to make sense. We aren't supposed to be able to explain it. It is beyond our understanding. This peace that protects our hearts and minds helps us navigate the world.

It is a knowing that somehow and some way everything will be okay, even when it feels like that is impossible. This peace is beyond anything that we can ever fully understand, study, or learn. We can read about it in Scripture and we can feel it over and over in our lives. Perhaps living it is our best shot at comprehending it.

How do you define the peace of God? What does it look and feel like for you? How does it guard your heart and mind every day?

_____

_____

_____

_____

_____

_____

_____

_____

_____

_____

_____

Day 77

God even knows how many hairs you have on your head. Don't be afraid. You are worth much more than many sparrows.

LUKE 12:7 NCV

D o you ever feel like God has forgotten you? When things are hard, it can feel like God is being silent or doesn't care about us at all. However, we don't have evidence to support this.

Our feelings are always accurate. Except sometimes, our feelings can lie to us. God will never forget us. God cares more for us than anything. Often when God is silent, it simply means He is actually really close and our pain is making it difficult to hear His voice. God knows us so well. He knows how many hairs we have on our heads. That's a lot of hairs to keep track of and He cares so much that He keeps track!

Luke 12:7 also says that we are worth much more to Him than the many sparrows. Every day God makes sure the sparrows find food, find mates, find their homes in the trees and birdhouses in our backyards. We can count on Him to provide for us too. Don't lose sight. Once again, which three words make up the second sentence in today's verse? Don't be afraid. We are going to *feel* our fear and move through it knowing He knows us well enough to know how many hairs we have, and we are worth more to Him than the many birds in the sky.

If God knows how many hairs are on your head, what else can you rest in knowing that He knows and sees about you?

_____

_____

_____

_____

_____

_____

_____

_____

_____

_____

Day 78

Even when I must walk through the darkest valley,
I fear no danger, for you are with me;
your rod and your staff reassure me.

PSALM 23:4 NET

There will always be times when your patience is not available. Maybe you snap and yell. In these moments, nothing is going right. You struggle to control your words, your feelings, and sometimes your actions. With anxiety, when your head is spinning with thoughts, your heart is beating too fast, or you can't catch your breath, it can feel like you're not in control. When you calm down and remember the things you can control, things begin to level out.

You can control how you react when things get dark in the valley. You can remember that God is with you. You can trust that somehow He will make it good. And for now, that means you can take a deep breath. Actually, take three of them. In through your nose, expand that belly big. Exhale through your nose or your mouth, and pull that belly button into your spine. Repeat. It may not feel like much, especially when there is so much in the dark valleys of life, but it is what we have. Breath and God's presence. It's enough.

How often do you remember to take deep breaths? What if you took three deep breaths first thing when you woke up, then set an alarm for after school to do them again, and then once more before you fall asleep?

_____

_____

_____

_____

_____

_____

_____

_____

_____

_____

_____

_____

Day 79

The name of the Lord is a strong tower;
the righteous man runs into it and is safe.

PROVERBS 18:10 ESV

Next time your anxiety is at a high level repeat Jesus' name. It might sound weird, but it's still worth trying. There is power in His name.

What if when you say Jesus, you are reminded that He lives in you? His grace, mercy, love, patience, joy, truth, and healing—living inside of you. What if when you say Jesus, you feel His overwhelming peace, love, and comfort? What if when you say Jesus, you invoke Holy Spirit in you to keep going?

I love that Proverbs 18:10 says that His name is a strong tower. Towers are high and they are strong to withstand the elements. When you say His name, what if it is as powerful as seeking shelter and refuge in a tower built to withstand life's greatest storms? Not only strong, but also high above the troubles? It is an image that makes me feel a bit safer, even if the only thing that is making me seek shelter is my anxiety. It is in His strength we are safe.

It is with His comfort that we feel that safety. Sometimes all we must remember is to run to Him.

If a tower isn't the image that helps you feel God's strength and comfort, what image does? Under His wings? In His fortress? Sitting beside Him? What else?

_____

_____

_____

_____

_____

_____

_____

_____

_____

_____

Day 80

The LORD will guide you continually,
giving you water when you are dry and restoring your strength.
You will be like a well-watered garden,
like an ever-flowing spring.

ISAIAH 58:11 NLT

I raise monarch butterflies. I started this hobby after one of the toughest seasons of my life. In that season, grief tried to swallow me whole into a pit of depression and anxiety. It was easy to be mad at God and forget how much He loves me.

I've always loved butterflies. They remind me of how resilient God's creations are, especially us. So, living in Missouri, right along the path the monarchs migrate, I planted a bunch of gardens full of nectar flowers for butterflies to drink from and milkweed for monarch caterpillars to eat and grow on. It was a reminder of God's character. He will always provide and He will always restore.

My gardens and the butterflies take work to maintain, just like the effort required when dealing with anxiety. I must water the garden in the heat of summer. I must weed the garden so the butterfly plants get the nutrients they need to grow. Through this care, the blooming of flowers, the growth of the black and yellow monarch caterpillars, and the flutter of the monarchs' black and orange wings, I see God's creativity, power, and love. Somehow, in this weird and cool hobby, God restores my strength and waters my soul.

Do you have a hobby? How does your hobby help you see God? If you don't have a hobby, what would you like to try?

_____

_____

_____

_____

_____

_____

_____

_____

_____

Day 81

Those who think they can do it on their own end up obsessed with measuring their own moral muscle but never get around to exercising it in real life.

ROMANS 8:5 MSG

Independence is important. Following through and showing up for yourself, especially with self-care, self-love, and self-acceptance, is part of a healthy life. With that in mind, too much independence is a not-so-great thing.

We are made for connection. We are neurobiologically wired to need one another. If we insist on doing everything ourselves because of pride or to avoid being a burden, we are choosing to not trust God. He wants us to rely on His Spirit in us.

Self-resilience, or the idea that we don't need each other, goes against how God made us. We need other people. So much goodness happens in connection, especially love and healing. Choosing independence to avoid being a burden often means we aren't allowing the people who love us most to love us well. Asking for help is hard because it requires vulnerability. I promise, the people who love us most want us to ask them for help—God included.

When is the last time you asked for help? Today, will you ask someone you trust for help on something, even if it's the tiniest favor. Write down how you've received help.

_____

_____

_____

_____

_____

_____

_____

_____

_____

_____

_____

_____

_____

Day 82

So now I live with the confidence that there is nothing in the universe with the power to separate us from God's love. I'm convinced that his love will triumph over death, life's troubles, fallen angels, or dark rulers in the heavens. There is nothing in our present or future circumstances that can weaken his love. There is no power above us or beneath us— no power that could ever be found in the universe that can distance us from God's passionate love, which is lavished upon us through our Lord Jesus, the Anointed One!

ROMANS 8:38–39 TPT

Nothing! Nothing can separate us from God's love. No thing. Nada. Zilch. Nothing.

Nothing we say or do. Nothing from our past. Nothing we do in the future. No lies we believe. No stories someone has told us about who we are. Nothing.

We are so loved that absolutely nothing can remove us from God's love.

What's even wilder? God loves us so much, He died for us.

That is a love like none other.

That is a love that changes everything.

Receive that love. Live that truth.

Live as truly loved as you are today.

Today's Scripture is a long one. Set a couple of alarms today to read these verses several times throughout the day. Really read these words, feel them in your bones, and know how much God loves you. Maybe write them out a few times. Put it up somewhere you can read it several times throughout the day. Remind yourself that there is no running from, escaping, or screwing up God's love for you.

Write down how you feel after reading Romans 8:38–39.

_____

_____

_____

_____

_____

_____

_____

_____

Day 83

The minute I said, "I'm slipping, I'm falling,"
your love, GOD, took hold and held me fast.

PSALM 94:18 MSG

God knows every single thing about you. He knew you and loved you before you were even born. And still, you must turn to Him and ask Him for help. You must tell Him how you feel. You must talk, listen, and be with Him throughout your days.

It is in these interactions with God that we build trust and a relationship with Him. When we turn to Him and ask for help, we're showing Him how much we trust Him. He is always ready. When we turn to Him we are reminded that His love never leaves us, never forsakes us, and is in us.

Are you in a season of being mad at God? Or ignoring Him? Or of yelling at Him? Can you remember the last time you asked Him for help? It's okay, He can handle it. Don't forget, sometimes we must remember to ask Him for help, then pause, and listen. Let God speak to you. What do you hear Him say?

Write down what you need help with and ask God. Then write down
how that surrender makes you feel.

_____

_____

_____

_____

_____

_____

_____

_____

_____

_____

_____

_____

_____

_____

Day 84

For God gave us a spirit not of fear but of
power and love and self-control.

2 TIMOTHY 1:7 ESV

When things feel chaotic and full of fear, it is comforting to know that God is not a God of chaos or fear. God is love. God is care. God is mercy. God is grace. For me, it isn't helpful to be scared of God's wrath. Yes, I will respect God, and more than that, I will revel and marvel in awe of Him. In awe of His power, His mercy, His grace, and most of all, His love.

Not only is God not a God of fear, He didn't give us a spirit of fear either. How could He when we read over and over throughout Scripture that He lives in us? God has given and gifted us with a spirit of power, love, and self-control. In some ways we could say that He has given us the spirit of courage. A force filled with love and the discipline to care for it well.

For me it feels easier to remember this God-given spirit when I am not running in fear of the God who loves me. Instead, I will sit in awe of His great love, turn to Him with my troubles, and remember who and what lives in me.

Have you been taught to be scared of God? How does this feel? What would it be like for you to think of that fear as awe and to remember how much God loves you?

_____

_____

_____

_____

_____

_____

_____

_____

_____

_____

Day 85

When I am in distress, I call to you, because you answer me.

PSALM 86:7

There are so many tools to help with anxiety. You can take deep breaths. You can spend time outside, feel the warmth of the sun, the grass under your feet, or the wind on your face. You can talk to someone you trust. You can play a song. You can dance it out. You can draw. You can watch a funny show. You can move your body. You can challenge your anxious thoughts. You can read Scripture. You can journal. You can talk to your therapist or pastor. You can read. You can practice gratitude. You can take a walk. You can spend time with your pet. There are so many ways you can cope with your anxiety in a healthy way.

Don't forget about one of the most powerful tools you have—God. Ask God for help. Share your anxious thinking with Him. Tell Him how unfair this feels. Question Him, praise Him, remind Him of His Word, take His promises as fact, ask Him to take it away and make it better.

Today, write something to God. Maybe even ask Him a question. Then wait and listen, and see what He says back. It might not be an audible voice. His response might feel more like a nudge or a random thought. Write it down and then ask Him, what do you need me to know today, Lord?

_____

_____

_____

_____

_____

_____

_____

_____

_____

_____

_____

_____

_____

_____

Day 86

For you are my hiding place; you protect me from trouble. You surround me with songs of victory.

PSALM 32:7 NLT

When I think of God as my hiding place, I am reminded of what it feels like to be in a blanket fort. Can you remember the last time you built a blanket fort? Draping whatever blankets or sheets you could find on top of tables, chairs, and couches. Then you'd crawl in with your favorite snack and book and feel the comfort and safety of this makeshift fort built from mismatched blankets and sheets. Inside you felt safe, protected, and comforted—all things I think God wants you to feel about who He is and what He provides for you. Maybe you brought a flashlight into your fort because you needed the reminder that there is always light in the dark. Jesus is that light always.

I suppose a blanket fort won't really protect you from actual danger—not like God will. It doesn't mean that hard things won't happen. God doesn't cause you pain, but He will sometimes allow it. In those times we must remember that He is our hiding place, kind of like a blanket fort. He surrounds us with songs of victory in that place. Victory songs because He will always work for good, even through the hard stuff He allows. Somehow it will be okay. We can trust that. Just like we can trust that building a blanket fort to hang out in will probably bring us some silly joy.

What do you think of when you read songs of victory and that God surrounds us with them? Today build a playlist filled with your own songs of victory. Make sure you play it, sing loudly to it, dance around in socked feet like your hips can feel the beat, even if they can't, and like no one is watching.

_____

_____

_____

_____

_____

_____

_____

Day 87

He consoles us as we endure the pain and hardship
of life so that we may draw from His comfort and
share it with others in their own struggles.

2 CORINTHIANS 1:4 VOICE

D o you have a "sit beside" friend? When you are going
through a difficult time, is there someone you love and
trust who when they see you struggling, sits beside you
with loving support? That's a "sit beside" friend. They
don't try to fix you or minimalize your sadness. They say
things like: I see you; I know this is hard; I don't know
what to say, I'm just glad you are telling me about your
struggles. I believe God, especially in the life of Jesus, is
the God of the "sit beside."

Sometimes a "sit beside" friend will say "me too; I've
felt this way before, it is brutal." This is empathy. I believe
empathy is a superpower. Empathy is to feel with someone, to sit beside them, to ask what it is like to live their
life and to believe them when they tell you. I think Jesus
did this over and over in Scripture. He really saw people.
He loved them well. He consoled them. He spoke truth in

love to them. He held them accountable for loving themselves and others well.

He is with us through it all. He will listen. He sees us. He has empathy for us. He knows what it is like to suffer. When we receive this love—His ability to be with us, especially in our suffering—we learn how to do it for others we care about. I'm not sure there is a more loving way to show people who Jesus is than to show them empathy like He has for us.

Sometimes the easiest way to get out of your own head and cope with your anxiety is to help someone. Showing up in a tangible way for someone who is really struggling is rewarding. Think of someone you care about who is in a tough season. How can you show up for them in a loving, empathic, and tangible way today?

_____

_____

_____

_____

_____

_____

Day 88

Come to me, all of you who are tired and have heavy loads, and I will give you rest.

MATTHEW 11:28 NCV

Does it ever feel like it is just too much? Too many activities, too much homework, too many people to please? Or maybe all the "not enough" feels like too much? When your anxiety is high everything feels like too much. Jesus said to bring it all to Him. Bring Him the too much and the not enough. It can all feel heavy and He can handle it for us. One of my favorite songs by United Pursuit begins with the lyrics:

> *Take a moment to remember*
> *Who God is and who I am*
> *There You go lifting my load again*

When we give the heavy and the too much over to Jesus, we are reminded that we aren't God. We aren't in charge of everything. We have a God who loves us so much He died for us. He sees us with the heavy load, in the too much and not enough, and loves us anyway. When we give Him the hard stuff, we can receive rest a little easier. I am talking about real rest. I don't mean Netflix-all-day rest. I'm talking about the "do nothing, be still, sit with yourself, listen to what God has to say, talk to Him, and give Him your heavy burdens" rest.

Set a timer for five to ten minutes to just sit and be still. No music, no videos, no phone, nothing. Just you and Jesus. After you're done, write down how the stillness made you feel.

_____

_____

_____

_____

_____

_____

_____

_____

Day 89

I cried out to the LORD in my great trouble, and he answered me.

JONAH 2:2 NLT

So much about anxiety and even about the world makes it easy for us to believe that we are alone. We're tricked into thinking that we must get over it, plow through it, and just be okay. It is truly one of the greatest lies society believes. The truth is, we are never alone. We are not the only ones to feel this way. We are not the only ones to go through something like this. When we believe the lie that we are alone, it is easy to believe that we must suffer alone. This isolated lie convinces us that reaching out for help is bothersome, even if we're reaching out to God.

Remember, He always knows anyway! Call out to Him. Ask for His presence. Ask for the miracle. "Ask and you shall receive" is what we are told. What would it be like if we actually lived our lives like that? What if the miracles, the love, and the community that we see in the Bible were actually still here today? Reach out to God, and please reach out to someone you trust. If they can't or won't help you, try again. I know it is scary and it takes courage to reach out to other people. You are worthy of it. You are not meant to do any of this alone.

When is the last time you asked for help? Have you asked God for help? How has He shown up for you?

_____

_____

_____

_____

_____

_____

_____

_____

_____

_____

_____

_____

_____

Day 90

He heals the brokenhearted and binds up their wounds.

PSALM 147:3

It's true that if you are brave enough to love, you will get hurt. Your heart will break many times throughout your life. Anxiety will tell you that the brokenness isn't worth it and that it is easier to just do it by yourself. Except that isn't true. To be brokenhearted means that you have allowed yourself to be seen and loved by someone else, which is a need we all have. You can also trust that God will be with you, that He will make it good and heal your broken heart.

If you ever twisted your ankle playing, your parents or the nurse probably wrapped your ankle, told you to elevate it, ice it, and stay off of it. Our loving Father binds up our hurts too. He assures us that His arms are strong enough to help us feel loved through the hurt. He holds us. He will make all things new and good for us, kind of like elevating the ankle. This verse is a promise and a truth. We can rely on it.

Have you been brokenhearted before? What helped you heal? How can you see God healing your broken heart?

_____

_____

_____

_____

_____

_____

_____

_____

_____

_____

_____

_____

_____

_____

_____

Day 91

Anxiety in the heart of man causes depression,
But a good word makes it glad.

PROVERBS 12:25 NKJV

When your brain feels anxious it can be exhausting.
Your ruminating thoughts are racing. You might fix-
ate on things while your heart is also racing. Fidgeting is
also very common. Anxiety can also be depressing, like
Proverbs 12:25 says. There will always be so much to
worry about. As I mentioned before, fear helps us to stay
safe. However, it is important to recognize that the level
of fear we feel in anxious times isn't the kind that we
need to keep us safe. It is the heightened level that makes
us unhappy.

Sometimes when I find myself worrying and my mood
is not great, I try to label my anxious thoughts. Is it a
to-do? Is it a worry? Is it dress-rehearsing? Is it catastro-
phizing? I label it and then I envision it passing through
my brain. I refocus my thoughts on something else, like
taking a deep breath, counting how many shades of green
I see, or checking in with my senses. What do I see? What

do I hear? What do I smell? What do I feel? What do I taste? These are ways to be present and to take the power away from anxious thinking.

Oh, and that "good word" is joy. We have joy with us always because we have Holy Spirit in us. Joy isn't the same as happy. Some days, happy is a choice. Some days it takes work. Joy though, joy is just there. Sometimes we simply must remember it.

How is your anxiety showing up lately? Worrying? Dress-rehearsing? Panic? Lists? Something else? Write down mindfulness practices to help you challenge it. Revisit this list next time your anxiety causes you to be depressed.

_____

_____

_____

_____

_____

_____

_____

Day 92

Your faith has made you well. Go in peace. Your suffering is over.

MARK 5:34 NLT

It's easy to forget that the healing Jesus did in the gospel wasn't some magical thing that only happened a super long time ago. Healing can and does happen today. In the case of today's verse, the faith of the bleeding woman coupled with her courage led her to Jesus. Often our healing will appear because we had the faith to believe it would *and* the courage to do something differently. Like asking for help, starting therapy, or beginning a routine in the morning to calm our anxiety.

There will also be times when we are doing all of the right things and it still doesn't work out. During these times, I find it helpful to remember how messy the world is and how fairness works. We must never put those characteristics on God. God is fair. God isn't messy. God will heal and, more than that, He became Jesus, lived, suffered, and died for us. Sometimes that means He allows unfair things to happen. Though when we have faith, we are made well. When we have faith, we have peace. When we have faith, our suffering is no more because we live loved and in the presence of God always.

Is there something you feel like you have the faith to be made better and it hasn't been? Have you allowed that to change who you know God to be? Today, write down a list of who you know God to be and who He tells us He is in Scripture.

_____

_____

_____

_____

_____

_____

_____

_____

_____

_____

_____

Day 93

You will forget your trouble
and remember it only as water gone by.

JOB 11:16 NCV

When we are in a tough season, it can feel hard to trust that there will be a day when we'll look back with different feelings. That we will one day maybe even be thankful for what we've been through. That those tough times brought us closer to God. That our faith grew. That we became a better person because of the struggle.

When we are in the struggle, we don't have this knowledge. It is okay to think, who cares, I just want things to get better and be easier. Have you said that to God yet? What if you prayed and asked God to give you some of that hindsight now? Building your faith in the dark is a reminder that troubles will fade.

I find it helpful to keep a list of those tough seasons throughout my life so I can later add all the goodness that has only come because of them. It's my "God is Faithful" list. I keep it on my phone and when things get tough, I read through this list of tough alongside the list of light.

I keep in mind that the light has only shone because of the list of darkness. The list of the light doesn't mean that the darkness wasn't hard; it means that we can trust that Jesus will bring light to any and everything.

I want you to make your own "God is Faithful" list. Write a list of your toughest seasons, challenges, and times. Alongside each item, write a list of the goodness you have because of those tough times. Add to this list and refer to it often. If you need more space, use the Notes section in the back.

_____

_____

_____

_____

_____

_____

_____

_____

_____

_____

Day 94

Look for the best in each other, and always
do your best to bring it out.

1 THESSALONIANS 5:15 MSG

It is hard to give what you don't have. If you aren't taking care of yourself, it will be hard to take care of others. It's the same for a lot of things in life. If you struggle to forgive yourself, it will be difficult to forgive others. If you don't love yourself well, it will be tough to love others well. If you don't extend grace and generosity to yourself, it will be hard to extend it to others. If you don't look for and believe the best in yourself, it will be very difficult to look for and believe the best about others.

Except right here in 1 Thessalonians, Paul the apostle told us not only to look for the best in each other, he also said to bring it out too. For me, this comes back to extending grace to ourselves and others. To assume positive intent. To live and know that we are all doing our best. Even when you are making a mistake, it is the best that you have in that given moment. If you knew better, you would have chosen better. Sometimes our best means we actually make a mistake. This is where you get to circle back, make it right, and begin again. Sometimes someone else's best isn't good enough for you and you must learn how to set boundaries. This is how you learn, grow, and change. You must make mistakes, learn, and begin again. When you assume the best in yourself and in others, the levels of difficulty and pain are reduced.

Do you look for the best in yourself? How can you extend grace toward yourself? What are some ways you can extend grace to someone else?

_____

_____

_____

_____

_____

_____

_____

_____

_____

Day 95

If we live in the Spirit, let us also walk in the Spirit. Let us not become conceited, provoking one another, envying one another.

GALATIANS 5:25–26 NKJV

What does the Bible mean by Spirit? The Greek word means wind, breath, spirit. The word is used in the Bible to describe and name Holy Spirit.

Who is Holy Spirit to you? It has helped me to stop saying "the Holy Spirit" because it felt like the term was making Holy Spirit seem less personal, and Spirit is a person. Holy Spirit lives in us and through us. Spirit is a helper and an advocate. Spirit is who we read in the Scriptures, especially earlier in Galatians, of the fruit of love, joy, peace, patience, kindness, goodness, faithfulness, gentleness, and self-control. Spirit is this fruit in and through us.

When I remember that this part of the Trinity lives in me—who Jesus tells us Holy Spirit is—and trust what the fruit of the Spirit is, it feels easier to live in, live from, and walk in Spirit. Maybe this is what it means when we hear others say to be more like Christ.

Who is Holy Spirit to you? How do you walk in Spirit every day? What fruit of the Spirit do you need more of right now?

_____

_____

_____

_____

_____

_____

_____

_____

_____

_____

_____

_____

_____

Day 96

Love your enemies, do good to those who hate you.

LUKE 6:27 NKJV

Anxiety can sometimes tell us that it is easier to live in either/ors and with labels. We're tricked into thinking things are all good or all bad. Anxiety tells us that life and people exist in only two categories. But the world is way messier than that and people are complicated. There are more than two sides. In life, there aren't just people who will be your best friends or your enemies. Every so often life occasionally throws you a curve ball and those people you thought were enemies actually become your friends.

When Jesus told us in Luke to love our enemies and then doubled down by saying to do good to those who hate us, it can feel like a bit of a gut punch. Others aren't good to us and still He told us to be good to them. It feels very counterintuitive. Except, in the upside-down world of Jesus, it isn't. Jesus gave us example after example in Scripture of how to love our enemies. To come alongside them and do good, even though they may persecute us.

For me, I find it helpful to remember that every single

person on earth is a creation of God. Every person is created in His image and with His likeness. If you hate your enemies, you are hating those created in His image. Plus, it will be hard to love them well like Jesus wants us to if we aren't doing good to or for them. Now, keep in mind, from time to time good needs to come from afar because some people aren't healthy for you. So sometimes doing good for your enemies simply means praying for them.

Is there someone you are struggling with lately? How can you pray for them? Is there someone you've realized the good needs to be directed toward from afar? How has the distance helped your well-being?

_____

_____

_____

_____

_____

_____

_____

_____

Day 97

Those who promote peace have joy.

PROVERBS 12:20

Today's verse seems so simple. Then why does it feel so hard to do, especially when we are struggling with anxiety? When anxiety is high and it feels like there is so much to worry about and to do, God wants us to promote peace, because if we can then we will have joy. What about our to-do lists and all these worries? Where do those go?

Occasionally, it can feel like Scripture verses are counterintuitive or impossible to uphold. When that happens, I find it helpful to look up the original text and identify what the words mean. In today's verse the word promote, in Hebrew, means to advise or resolve. The word peace, in Hebrew, means safe, well, happy, friendly, welfare, health, prosperity, and peace. Researching the meaning helps me create a reader-friendly version of the verse. If I advise and resolve to be happy and friendly, I will have joy. Well, what about joy? The word joy, in Hebrew, means glee. I love that! Who doesn't need more glee in their life?

Here's the deal though. We have peace always because we have Jesus. It can be easy to forget or not feel that peace with everything going on in the world, and in our heads. So, we will have to advise and resolve or promote peace at times, and in doing so we'll have more glee.

How do you describe peace? What about joy? When is the last time you felt these? How can you feel them today?

_____

_____

_____

_____

_____

_____

_____

_____

_____

_____

Day 98

Love patiently accepts all things. It always trusts,
always hopes, and always endures.

1 CORINTHIANS 13:7 NCV

Let's try something a little different with today's verse.
Read it a couple of times with two different lenses for love.

Read first as love. Love like the feeling. Healthy love
is patient and trusts and hopes and endures. I say healthy
love because sometimes there are things we do not need to
be accepting of because they aren't safe or healthy.

Now read love as in Jesus as love because Jesus is
Love. Jesus is patient, trusts, hopes, and always endures.
It can sometimes feel difficult to wrap our heads around
the life, suffering, death, and resurrection of Jesus.

At times, our heads try to make worldly sense of Jesus
as love, when in fact there will always be some of our faith
that isn't easily understood. Most of the time, that's how I
feel about the love Jesus has for us. He suffered and gave
so much for us. He loved us so much He chose the cross
for us. At the end of the day, it comes back to love. Jesus
as love. Jesus is love. Love. And love always endures.

Have you ever thought of Jesus in this way? How would your
relationship with God change if you thought of Him more as love?

_____

_____

_____

_____

_____

_____

_____

_____

_____

_____

_____

_____

_____

Day 99

Now the Lord is the Spirit, and where the Spirit of the Lord is, there is freedom.

2 CORINTHIANS 3:17

Spirit lives in us. Jesus said so. That means freedom lives in us. We don't have to be our anxiety, our mistakes, or who we think we should be or who we have been told we have to be, for that matter. We have Jesus; therefore, we are free. Knowing this gives me strength and hope. Whether in fun times or hard times, we can trust that Spirit is in us, so freedom is in us.

What if you reminded your anxiety of that when it says you can't breathe, when it tries to force you to do something to be okay, or when you struggle to fall asleep? Imagine yourself standing up to it and saying, "Excuse me anxiety, I need you to remember that God lives in me, which means I have freedom, peace, joy, contentment, faith, and trust."

Friend, this is where you tell your anxiety your truth through Jesus. Where you feel that anxiety and refuse to be it by leaning into the truth you have in and through

Christ. And just in case you need help today, that truth is something like: I am loved. I am chosen. I am free.

If you have God in you, what else can you trust is in you? How can you tell your anxiety these truths when it tries to make you anxious?

_____

_____

_____

_____

_____

_____

_____

_____

_____

_____

_____

_____

Day 100

I will be with you, day after day, to the end of the age.

MATTHEW 28:20 VOICE

Day after day, minute after minute, breath after breath, in each step, and in every thought, God is with you. Before you were born until the end of the age, God not only knows and sees you, He is with you through it all.

When He feels distant and quiet, that usually means He is nearest. Sing in His shadow. Open your eyes and see Him in all of the things around you. Take a breath and feel His Spirit in you. Close your eyes and know God loves you. God will never leave you. God will always be with you. He will make everything good and for your good. He loves you more than you can imagine, anxiety and all. Live as loved as you are.

I am so proud of you and so grateful that God connected us. This one-hundred-day journey is the first step to dealing with anxiety. This devotional is a resource and I hope you've learned new tools and methods to use when your anxiety stirs up. I hope you've deepened your faith and your relationship with God. Thank you for allowing me to walk alongside you.

This isn't the end of our time together—you can reread the devotional, memorize the Scripture verses, and expand on the journaling prompts. Today, I want you to relish in your hard work and courage. Write down some of the biggest lessons you've learned through our time together. When you're feeling down and anxious, revisit the learnings you've written and remember how loved you are and that you're never alone.

_____

_____

_____

_____

_____

_____

_____

_____

_____

_____

_____

_____

Notes

Notes

Notes

Notes

Notes

Notes

Notes

Notes

Notes

Notes